SCHOLASTIC

D0743672

QAR
Comprehension Lessons

Grades
4–5

Laura S. Pardo
Taffy E. Raphael
Kathryn H. Au

New York • Toronto • London • Auckland • Sydney
Mexico City • New Delhi • Hong Kong • Buenos Aires

Teaching *Resources*

We appreciate the hard work and contributions of Kari Corsi, Elizabeth Strode, Amy Waechter-Versaw, and Jo Parker to the process of creating the QAR Comprehension Lessons series. We also thank Sarah Glasscock for her stellar editorial work.

Taffy Raphael and Kathy Au
May 2011

Permission credits appear on page 128.

Development editor: Sarah Longhi

Editor: Sarah Glasscock

Copy editor: David Klein

Cover designer: Maria Lilja

Cover photography: Maria Lilja

Interior designer: Melinda Belter

Interior illustrations: Kathie Kelleher

ISBN: 978-0-545-26410-5

Contents

Introduction

BY TAFFY E. RAPHAEL AND KATHRYN H. AU

QAR—Question Answer Relationships—is a categorization system detailing the relationship among a question, the text to which the question refers, and the reader's knowledge base. It can serve as a framework for comprehension instruction, as well as a pedagogical tool for improving teachers' and students' questioning abilities.

The *QAR Comprehension Lessons* books are designed to support teachers who wish to improve comprehension instruction in their classroom, teams of teachers within grade levels or departments who wish to build coherence into their comprehension instruction, and school staff members who are developing a coherent staircase comprehension curriculum. Current initiatives, such as widespread adoption of the Common Core State Standards, emphasize comprehension in learning across the disciplines and highlight the importance of helping all students reach high levels of achievement. Yet teaching comprehension and critical thinking about text, the *raison d'être* for reading, has challenged literacy educators for decades.

Although comprehension is one of the most critical outcomes for literacy instruction, teachers and students can't see, touch, or examine it directly. Comprehension is famously elusive, and our goal in these books is to demystify its instruction.

Comprehension Strategies

Readers use an array of comprehension strategies to construct the author's intended meaning (see Israel & Duffy, 2009). But what comprehension strategies should teachers focus on? Table 1 details similarities and variations in how comprehension has been described in widely cited reviews of research (e.g., Dole, Duffy, Roehler, & Pearson, 1991) and popular professional literature (e.g., Fountas & Pinnell, 2001; Hoyt, 2005). Our understanding of the research led us to emphasize the six strategies shown in the Table 1.

In *QAR Comprehension Lessons* we teach routines to support comprehension through predicting, drawing inferences, identifying important information, summarizing, questioning, and monitoring. Despite slight variations in the way researchers have categorized comprehension strategies, these strategies and our approach to teaching them (see Au & Raphael, 2010; Raphael, & Au, in press; Raphael et al., 2009) align with those of other contemporary literacy educators and researchers (e.g., Dole et al., 1991; Fountas & Pinnell, 2001; Harvey & Goudvis, 2007; Hoyt, 2005; McLaughlin & Allen, 2009).

TABLE 1 A Comparison of Comprehension Categories

QAR STRATEGY FOCUS	DOLE ET AL. (1991)	FOUNTAS & PINNELL (2001)	HOYT (2005)	HARVEY & GOUDVIS (2007)	MCLAUGHLIN & ALLEN (2009)
Predicting	Predicting	Predicting	Predicting Creating images	Activating background knowledge Visualizing	Predicting Previewing Visualizing
Drawing Inferences	Drawing Inferences	Inferring Connecting Analyzing Critiquing	Inferring Connecting Using analogy	Making Inferences Visualizing	Inferring Visualizing
Identifying Important Information	Identifying Important Information	Gathering	Determining Importance Skimming Scanning		Identifying
Summarizing	Summarizing	Summarizing Synthesizing	Summarizing Paraphrasing Comparing	Synthesizing	Reconstructing
Questioning	Questioning		Self-Questioning		Self-Questioning
Monitoring	Monitoring	Monitoring			Evaluating Judging

Table 2 below provides what we regard as reasonable definitions and purposes for these strategies, and their relationship to specific QARs.

TABLE 2 Defining Comprehension Strategies

QAR	COMPREHENSION STRATEGY	DEFINITION
Author & Me	Predicting	Using text information and background knowledge and experience to create a hypothesis that anticipates what is going to occur in the text
Author & Me	Drawing Inferences	Constructing ideas and interpretations using information that is not explicitly stated in the text
Right There * Think & Search	Identifying Important Information	Sorting the essential from non-essential content to achieve the purpose(s) for reading
Right There * Think & Search	Summarizing	Creating a brief coherent text from the essential content of the original source
Author & Me	Questioning	Raising and responding to queries whether explicit or implied
Author & Me	Monitoring	Being aware of the quality and degree of understanding and knowing how to address comprehension breakdowns

The content, structure, and format of the lessons presented in this book reflect four fundamental elements.

1. Comprehension instruction begins with the building of a shared language for discussing comprehension strategies and challenges.

2. Lessons are framed in terms of the reading cycle that reflects readers' stances before, during, and after reading.

3. Specific comprehension strategies or combinations of strategies are taught within the context of the reading cycle, using the language of QAR.

4. Lessons across the three books (grades 2–3, grades 4–5, grades 6–8) are parallel. For example, Lesson 14 always focuses on questioning with narrative text. However, the routines and tools taught within the lesson reflect a developmental approach to curriculum, with texts becoming more challenging, and strategies more sophisticated, as students move up the grades.

QAR: A Shared Language
for Comprehension Instruction

A shared language for discussing the information sources used to construct meaning is central to the *QAR Comprehension Lessons* books. QAR provides the shared language to be used by both teachers and students. As a shared language, QAR can connect strategy instruction across content areas within a classroom, classrooms within a grade level, and grade levels across a whole school (Raphael, Highfield, & Au, 2006). It gives teachers greater precision in conveying complex concepts associated with comprehension, such as where knowledge comes from; relationships among questions or purposes for reading, text, and readers' knowledge; and relationships among strategies and their use across the curriculum. The QAR language also gives teachers a means to model and think aloud about comprehension with their students. Once students learn the language of QAR, they are better able to describe and discuss the comprehension problems they are encountering.

Learning the four core QARs is a first step for teachers and students. But the value of QAR comes from students and teachers using its language to explain their thinking while working to comprehend text. Since questions are central to establishing purposes for engaging with all kinds of text, the vocabulary helps teachers and students communicate about questions (i.e., purposes for reading) and their relationship to various sources of information. It guides them in determining the most useful or appropriate sources of information for accessing or constructing answers to the questions. Figure 1 displays the basic vocabulary of QAR, which consists of three paired comparisons. This vocabulary remains consistent regardless of students' age levels, reading abilities, or dispositions.

FIGURE 1

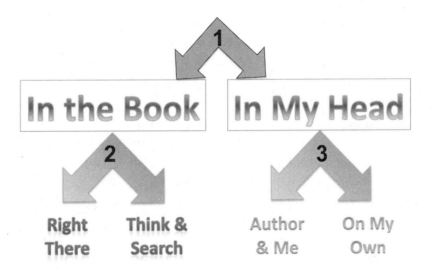

The First Paired Comparison:
In the Book/In My Head

The first paired comparison introduces students to the metaphors of "head" and "book." The terms distinguish between information external to the text source (*In My Head*) or internal to the text source (*In the Book*). The term *head* refers to the reader's knowledge and life experiences (i.e., prior or background knowledge). The term *book* stands for all kinds of texts: conventional print materials, including books, magazines, and newspapers; digital formats such as Web pages and blogs; and graphic images, including charts, graphs, and video. Evidence of learning can be seen when new In the Book information acquired today becomes In My Head, background information tomorrow. With these broad distinctions in mind, think about the information sources needed to answer each of the following questions about a story that describes a highly unusual set of events at a youngster's birthday party:

▶ What is the most unusual birthday party you've ever attended?

▶ What were the things about Ellie's birthday party that surprised Nate?

The first question does not require readers to have understood the story or even to have read it. There are many possible answers since readers likely have a range of birthday party experiences and different criteria for what constitutes "unusual." In contrast, to answer the second question, readers must understand sufficient information from the text to distinguish unexpected from expected features of the party. The first question is an In My Head QAR; the second, an In the Book (Raphael et al., 2006; Raphael & Au, in press).

The Second Paired Comparison:
Right There/Think & Search

The second paired comparison distinguishes between the two In the Book QARs: Right There and Think & Search. These QARs differ in terms of the *place(s)* in the text in which students can find relevant information for answering the question. With Right There QARs, all the information needed to answer a question is in *one place* within the text. With Think & Search QARs, the reader must search across *multiple places* to construct a complete answer. As readers mature, the definition of *place* will change. In the primary grades, *same place* refers to a single sentence. In the intermediate grades, students generally consider *same place* to be within a single paragraph. By middle school and beyond, readers generally consider *same place* to encompass a larger amount of text—sections, chapters, or when using text sets, an entire book.

Place, in the language of QAR, must remain fluid. For example, students in one fourth-grade classroom noted that a question didn't seem like a Think & Search QAR when they were simply looking at different sentences in the same paragraph. Their teacher agreed, and collaboratively, they decided that they would define *same place* as within a single paragraph. In other cases, the teacher, rather than the students, raised the possibility of expanding the definition of place. We have found that it rarely matters who brings it up, as long as students are ready to reconsider how place is defined to distinguish between Right There and Think & Search QARs.

The Third Paired Comparison: Author & Me/On My Own

The third paired comparison expands In My Head QARs into two categories: Author & Me and On My Own. Both QARs involve questions that require readers to respond using information from their own background knowledge and life experiences. The distinction between the two comes down to the amount of significant, actionable information the reader uses from the text to determine the appropriate background knowledge to access.

On My Own QARs require little or no information from the text for readers to construct a complete and appropriate answer. These QARs are designed to build the reader's knowledge prior to reading or to draw on the reader's experience during the reading process. Author and Me QARs build a bridge between the cognitive strategy or strategies students use to construct the author's intended meaning and personal responses they create to make text-to-self and self-to-text connections. While the information used to answer the question comes from the reader's own knowledge base and life experiences, knowing *what* to access and *why* involves understanding the text. Author & Me QARs underscore the connection between the text and reader's world.

Together, the language of QAR provides a way of talking about the relationships among the purposes for reading, the questions readers are asked or ask themselves, the text source(s), and the readers' knowledge base. When used in the context of comprehension strategy instruction, QAR language can make visible the role of particular strategies in responding to different QARs.

QARs and The Reading Cycle

A second fundamental element of the *QAR Comprehension Lessons* books is the emphasis on how the language of QAR can provide a way to talk about the information sources readers use within the reading cycle, as depicted in Figure 2.

FIGURE 2

BEFORE READING: When drawing on background knowledge (other texts by the same author, similar genres or topics, and so on), teachers and students engage in conversation driven by On My Own QARs as they prepare to enter the text world. A reader who has read part of the text, put it aside, and is now returning to it, or a reader using significant information from the text (e.g., table of contents, headings, charts, images) draws on Author & Me QARs, building from previous readings to anticipate or make predictions about ideas and events before entering the text world.

DURING READING: The dominant QARs are Think & Search and Author & Me, with the occasional Right There QAR asked and answered to highlight important ideas and details. As readers move through the text, they use all the resources they can muster to make sense of what they are reading: identifying key information (Right There or Think & Search), making inferences (Author & Me), summarizing (Think & Search), monitoring to check predictions (Author & Me), and so forth. In effect, they are making text-to-self connections that facilitate meaning construction. However, while in the text world, they also step back and reflect on how content is changing their knowledge and perceptions—not only of the text world, but also of their own world. As they reflect, they invoke a range of reader responses (Author & Me) that enhance their engagement with the text.

AFTER READING: Upon leaving the text world, readers respond critically to what they have read, using strategies that support Author & Me QARs. For example, they revisit characters' motivations and how plots have played out. Stories may change the way readers think about aspects of their own lives. They engage in critical analysis of the quality of the text, moving beyond whether or not the text was a "good read" ("I liked this because . . ." "This was useful because . . .") to considering the strengths and weaknesses of the narrative, the argument, or information presented.

Understanding the reading cycle and the QARs associated with each phase of the cycle helps readers in several ways. It enables readers to connect the stances they assume toward the text before, during, and after reading; recognize the QARs (knowledge sources) they should draw on during each phase of the cycle; and identify the comprehension strategies useful at various times.

Core Comprehension Strategies

The third fundamental element of the *QAR Comprehension Lessons* is the use of QAR language in teaching students about, and modeling routines for, successful comprehension. Lessons model tools that support cognitive engagement in each of the six comprehension strategies defined in Table 2 on page 6. The QAR language and lessons enrich students' understanding of what it means to be an active, strategic reader.

Predicting

Predicting, an Author & Me QAR, requires readers to use what they know, shaped by information provided by the text. Before reading, the text information may simply be the title or genre or name of the author that readers use to construct their image of the text world that they are about to enter. During reading, the author provides clues that readers use to consider what will happen next. Ideas for the prediction must, by definition, come from the readers' head (i.e., Me), though the text (i.e., Author) provides important clues about what might be relevant.

Drawing Inferences

Like predicting, drawing inferences is an Author & Me QAR, requiring readers to use text information to guide them as they seek relevant ideas and information from their heads. Readers draw inferences "to arrive at a decision or opinion by reasoning from known facts or evidence" (Fountas & Pinnell, 2001, p. 317). Their decision or opinion comes from their heads, but it is constrained by clues from the author.

Identifying Important Information

Identifying important information requires routines that can be used to answer Think & Search and Right There QARs as readers separate essential from nonessential text content. The important information is In the Book, requiring that readers either Think & Search the text, or if the important information is a single detail, find it Right There in one place.

Summarizing

Summarizing, primarily a Think & Search QAR, builds on the foundation established by identifying important information. Readers reorganize the important information to construct a brief, coherent version of the completed text. Summarizing may reflect Author & Me QAR routines when readers bring their own opinions, warranted by the text, into the condensed version.

Questioning

QARs related to questioning depend on who asks the question. When readers answer questions posed by others (e.g., peers, their teacher, textbooks), they use routines appropriate to the likely QAR. When readers generate questions, Author & Me QARs are most relevant since readers must stay consistent with the text content (Author) while they go beyond the text (Me) to create the question. They cannot generate text-based questions unless they have already read the text, and they have little reason to generate On My Own QARs as these play a lesser role in comprehension instruction during and after reading.

Comprehension Monitoring

Monitoring, like questioning, is primarily Author & Me since readers are engaged in an ongoing process of inquiry about the text. Capable, active readers—when monitoring—are checking their success in accurately predicting, drawing inferences, asking questions, figuring out the important information, and creating accurate summaries. They respond to breakdowns in comprehension by using their own knowledge, guided and shaped by the information the author has provided.

Strategies in Combination

Active readers neither choose a text based on using a given strategy (e.g., so they can summarize or predict), nor use strategies one at a time. They invoke comprehension strategies based on need, usually finding some more useful than others, depending on the phase in the reading cycle (e.g., predicting before reading, summarizing after reading). When students know which strategies are useful for particular QARs, and which QARs are likely to arise at different parts of the reading cycle, they are in a position to understand how to be active and strategic, invoking strategies appropriate to the reading process that can improve their understanding of text.

A Multiyear Approach

The fourth element in *QAR Comprehension Lessons* reflects the importance of a coherent multiyear approach. One year of comprehension instruction is rarely sufficient, even when provided by a highly skilled and experienced teacher who has implemented the shared language of QAR. Further, texts increase in complexity from primary grades to middle school, and students benefit from practice extending their knowledge of strategies to new and more complex situations, while learning new tools to support their comprehension of more challenging texts. In our experience, the importance of a multiyear approach holds across all schools. However, it is especially salient in schools serving a high proportion of students who struggle with reading and writing. These students definitely require two, three, or more years of coherent instruction in comprehension instruction—the more, the better.

Coherence is at the heart of what Kathy Au (Au & Raphael, 2011) describes as a *staircase curriculum*. The staircase curriculum is one in which teachers hold a clear vision of the excellent graduating reader and writer—the top step. At each grade level, teachers have a clear understanding of the goals their students must achieve to climb the staircase and achieve this vision. Each stair is steep enough to ensure progress, and there are no cracks in the staircase through which a student might fall.

QAR Comprehension Lessons embodies the concept of the staircase curriculum. Within and across books, the goal is to help students and their teachers develop and use a shared language for talking about comprehension strategy use throughout the reading cycle. Thus, initial lessons focus on introducing the QAR language. Then the QAR language is connected to the reading cycle. Next, lessons focus on the link between strategy use and traversing the reading cycle successfully. Fourth, lessons teach students the formal metacognitive strategy of monitoring this process to support understanding.

Across the books, steps "rise" in terms of text difficulty, routines taught, and balance between oral and written activity. For example, comprehension strategies that involve only a few parts (e.g., predicting) are taught in similar ways across the books, with the staircase reflected in text difficulty and the range of tools introduced to students. With strategies involving multiple parts (e.g., summarizing, monitoring), the lessons differ across the books. Lessons for younger students reflect more collaborative oral work and focus on basic routines or tools readers use. Lessons in the upper grades provide an expanded repertoire of tools and promote increasing independence in applying the tools to more complex texts.

Organization of the QAR Comprehension Lessons Books

The three books in the *QAR Comprehension Lessons* series are designed for use at primary grades (2–3), intermediate grades (4–5), and middle school (6–8). Each book is organized into four sections:

SECTION 1: Lessons 1–3 introduce students to the basic concepts and vocabulary of QAR.

SECTION 2: Lesson 4 connects QAR language to the before, during, and after stages of the reading cycle.

SECTION 3: Lessons 5–14 focus on the five core comprehension strategies. These lessons use QAR language to teach students basic routines and tools for predicting, drawing inferences, identifying important information, summarizing, and questioning in informational and narrative texts.

SECTION 4: Lessons 15 and 16 focus on comprehension monitoring. These lessons help students understand how active readers use the strategies, routines, and tools discussed in Lessons 1–14 to monitor their understanding and invoke relevant solutions in response to comprehension problems in informational and narrative text.

Each lesson moves through the six steps of the gradual release of responsibility instructional model (Pearson, 1985): explicit explanation, modeling, coaching, guided practice, independent application, and self-assessment and goal setting. A lesson can be taught in one extended session but is designed to be taught easily over two days: Day 1 from Explicit Explanation through Guided Practice and Day 2 from Coaching to Self-Assessment & Goal-Setting. An informational or narrative passage accompanies each lesson and is annotated to show which section to use with each step. Sample think-alouds in each lesson show how you might introduce the appropriate QAR and demonstrate its application with the passage as you move from explicit explanation to promoting students' independent application. On the accompanying CD, you'll find whole-class posters and charts to use during instruction and for students' reference during and beyond the lesson; charts and graphics for students to use in small groups, pairs, and individually (or as models to copy onto their own notebook paper); and the passages to copy for student use. These passages provide a balance between informational texts with science, social studies, and mathematics content, and narrative text and poetry, including stories and biographies.

Concluding Comments

We hope that these lessons show that comprehension and comprehension instruction need not be elusive. We have designed them to help teachers navigate the complexities of comprehension instruction. At one level, the lessons are models of how instruction can be scaffolded to move students toward independent application of what they have been taught. At another level, the lessons are models for comprehension instruction of core strategies that research has demonstrated to be central to meaning-making. At yet another level, the lessons provide a window into different grouping arrangements to support student-to-student discussion in pairs and small groups. At their core, the lessons demonstrate how QAR, as a language of instruction, can lead students to take control of their reading processes and gain a deeper understanding of text.

References

Au, K. H., & T. E. Raphael (2010). Using workshop approaches to support the literacy development of English language learners. In G. Li, & P. A. Edwards (Eds.). *Best Practices in ELL Instruction* (pp. 207–221). New York: Guilford.

Au, K. H., & Raphael, T. E. (2011). Building a staircase curriculum. *New England Journal of Reading, 46*(2), 1-8.

Dole, J. A., Duffy, G. G., Roehler, L. R., & Pearson, P. D. (1991). Moving from the old to the new: Research on reading comprehension instruction. *Review of Educational Research, 61*(2), 239–264.

Fountas, I., & Pinnell, G. S. (2001). *Guiding Readers and Writers, Grades 3–6: Teaching Comprehension, Genre, and Content Literacy.* Westport, CT: Heinemann.

Harvey, S., & Goudvis, A. (2007). *Strategies that work.* Portland, MA: Stenhouse.

Hoyt, L. (2005). *Spotlight on comprehension: Building a literacy of thoughtfulness.* Westport, CT: Heinemann.

Israel, S. E. D., & Duffy, G. G.(Eds.). (2009). *Handbook of research on reading comprehension.* New York: Taylor & Francis.

McLaughlin, M., & Allen, M. B. (2009). *Guided comprehension in Grades 3–8* (2nd Ed.). Newark, DE: International Reading Association.

Pearson, P. D. (1985). Changing the face of reading comprehension instruction. *The Reading Teacher, 38*(6), 724–738.

Raphael, T. E., & Au, Kathryn H. (in press). In J. Paratore & R.L. McCormack (Eds.), *After Early Intervention: Then What?* (2nd Ed.). Newark, DE: International Reading Association.

Raphael, T. E., Highfield, K., & Au, K. H. (2006). *QAR now: A powerful and practical framework that develops comprehension and higher-level thinking in all students.* New York: Scholastic.

Raphael, T. E., George, M.A., Weber, C. M., & Nies, A. (2009). Approaches to teaching reading comprehension. In S. E. Israel & G. G. Duffy (Eds.), *Handbook of research on reading comprehension* (pp. 449–469). New York: Lawrence Erlbaum Associates, Taylor and Francis Group.

In the Book/In My Head QARs

GOAL • Introduce QAR language:
In the Book and In My Head

I Can Statement

I know the difference between In the Book and In My Head QARs and can use this knowledge to improve my comprehension.

Materials *(See CD for reproducibles.)*

▶ "Animal Keeper" by Judith Jango-Cohen (informational passage), p. 20 (one copy for each student)

▶ QAR Information Sources Poster (display copy)

▶ QAR Self-Assessment Thinksheet (one copy for each student)

BEFORE READING	DURING READING	AFTER READING

Step **1** EXPLICIT EXPLANATION

Tell students that today you will teach them how to recognize and identify the two sources of information for creating good answers to questions:

▶ The texts we read

▶ Our own background knowledge and experiences

Display the I Can Statement and have students read it aloud with you. Then introduce the concept:

> *We are going to learn about QARs today. QAR stands for Question Answer Relationships. When we seek to gain a good understanding of what we're reading, it's helpful to think of the different sources of information we can draw on. When I read, I ask myself questions to help me focus and think about the ideas in the texts. But questions arise in many different ways. Sometimes someone else asks me a question about what I read—like a friend who wants to know about what I'm reading or another teacher. Sometimes we ask*

ourselves questions, and sometimes questions are printed in the books or other materials we read.

When I read and answer questions, one source of information is In the Book or text I am reading. Another source is In My Head—from my own background knowledge and experiences. What you learn today about QAR will help you any time you read.

Show the QAR Information Sources Poster. Explain to students that it is important to think about these sources of information when they read. Good readers use both of these sources to make sense of what they read. When readers understand what they read, it helps them in many ways: learning new information, thinking about their own lives in new and different ways, and in asking and answering questions.

Emphasize again to students that questions arise in different ways: we're asked questions by others (you may wish to elicit examples of this from students), we ask questions of ourselves (again, you may wish to elicit students' experiences when they've asked themselves questions), and sometimes we find them printed in books or other materials we read.

DURING READING

Step **2** MODELING

Read aloud the title and first two paragraphs of "Animal Keeper." Then display the following questions:

▶ What does Hazel Davies do for a job? [*In the Book: manages animals in museum exhibits*]

▶ What do people do at a museum? [*In My Head: Answers will vary depending on students' experiences.*]

▶ Who or what is Iggy? [*In the Book: an iguana*]

Now that I have read the text, I am going to answer these questions. I need to remember that I will find the answers either In the Book or In My Head.

The first question asks me about Hazel Davies' job. I think this must be an In the Book QAR because the article describes how she works with lizards and snakes and other animals at a museum. I think the QAR for the second question can be an In My Head since I've gone to museums and know from my previous experiences how we walk around and see exhibits. The third question asks me about Iggy, which I know was described in the article, so the most helpful QAR here is to look In the Book for information.

Step 3 GUIDED PRACTICE

> *Now I want you to give it a try. I'm going to read the next section to you, "Going Live." Then I will ask you to use what you have learned about In the Book and In My Head QARs to help me answer three more questions.*

Read aloud the two paragraphs in the "Going Live" section. Then display the following questions:

▶ What are butterflies like? [*In My Head: Answers will vary depending on students' experiences.*]

▶ What is the Butterfly Conservatory at the American Museum of Natural History? [*In the Book: The Conservatory displays hundreds of live butterflies.*]

▶ Where does the museum get the butterflies? [*In the Book: from butterfly farms around the world*]

Guide students to use what they have learned about the two types of QARs to identify appropriate information for answering the questions.

Step 4 COACHING

Hand out a copy of "Animal Keeper" to each student. Have them read the next section, "Critter Care."

> *Now you will use what you learned about In the Book and In My Head QARs as you work with a partner to answer two questions. First, determine whether the QAR for each question is an In the Book or In My Head. Next, write the answer to each question. Finally, be prepared to show where you found the answer to In the Book QARs and what knowledge or experiences you drew on for In My Head QARs.*

While students work, monitor and facilitate their use of the two core QARs. Provide additional support as needed. As students begin to finish the reading, display the following questions:

▶ In the museum, what do butterflies eat? [*In the Book: sugary sweet nectar*]

▶ What is an interesting or unusual animal you would like to feed? [*In My Head: Answers will vary based on students' interests.*]

When students have completed the task, ask them to share the QARs that guided their question answering, explain their answers, and show or describe the evidence they drew on.

Step **5** INDEPENDENT APPLICATION

> *You are getting good at using QAR knowledge to improve your comprehension. Now I want you to use QAR on your own. Please read the final section, "A Great Career." Then think about whether the information you need to answer each question is an In the Book or In My Head QAR. For each question, indicate the type of QAR, the answer, and be prepared to share your evidence.*

While students are reading, display the following questions:

- ▶ What does Davies feed the Water Monitor? [*In the Book: dangles a rat for the Water Monitor to find*]

- ▶ Would you like to have a job like Davies' in the future? Why or why not? [*In My Head: Answers will vary according to students' interests and experiences.*]

- ▶ What other kinds of animals live in cages? [*In My Head: Answers will vary according to students' interests and experiences.*]

- ▶ What kind of lizard eats crickets and jumped on Davies' face? [*In the Book: a leaftailed gecko*]

BEFORE READING   DURING READING   **AFTER READING**

Step **6** SELF-ASSESSMENT & GOAL SETTING

Allow several students to share their answers and evidence. Then return their focus to the goal of the lesson in preparation for completing the QAR Self-Assessment Thinksheet. Revisit the I Can Statement:

> *I know the difference between In the Book and In My Head QARs and can use this knowledge to improve my comprehension.*

Remind students that understanding QARs can support their understanding of text and help them in answering questions.

> *Now I would like you to think about how you can use this strategy in other areas and how you can add it to your own personal toolkit for reading.*

Have students complete a QAR Self-Assessment Thinksheet and turn it in with the answers to the final four questions.

Animal Keeper

By Judith Jango-Cohen

For use with
Step 2: Modeling
title and
introduction

When Hazel Davies goes to work, she is greeted by leaping lizards, curious snakes, and tortoises that mistake her green sneakers for snacks. Although it might sound like Davies works at a zoo, she's actually in charge of managing the animals that star in exhibitions at the American Museum of Natural History in New York City.

The live exhibits feature a colorful cast of creatures, from blue butterflies and red frogs to a green iguana nicknamed "Iggy." Museum visitors enjoy live-action attractions because the animals add an element of surprise to displays. But an animal needs more than a cute face or bright colors to earn a spot in an exhibition hall.

Going Live

For use with
Step 3:
Guided Practice
"Going Live"
section

Curators at the museum carefully choose animals that will help bring to life an important concept in an exhibit. For example, for *The Butterfly Conservatory*, which explores the importance of butterflies in the web of life, curators decided to include hundreds of live butterflies. Every fall, in preparation for the butterfly exhibition, Davies imports hundreds of these insects by working with butterfly farms around the world. When the butterflies arrive, Davies releases them into an artificial habitat that visitors can enter. There, humans and butterflies mingle—which the museum hopes gives visitors a deeper appreciation of these delicate insects.

Bringing butterflies—or any other type of animal—into an exhibition requires detailed research, says Davies. Staff at the museum must first find out if the animal they want to showcase is available from breeders. That is important because the museum wants to minimize the collection of wild animals.

Critter Care

For use with
Step 4: Coaching
"Critter Care"
section

Davies and her staff must also research whether the museum can stock the proper food for the various animals. Storing sugary-sweet nectar for butterflies is simple enough, but some critters have more complicated cravings.

For their exhibition, *Frogs: A Chorus of Colors*, the museum showcased 67 dart poison frogs. In the wild, the frogs eat toxic ants that allow the amphibians to release poison from their skin. Since the museum did not want poisonous animals wandering around their display cases, a meal of their favorite ants was not an option for the frogs. Instead, Davies fed the dart poison frogs fruit flies, crickets, and wax worms. That way she rendered the amphibians harmless. "They got [all the nutrients] they needed from what we fed them," says Davies. "But it's safer to handle them when they're not poisonous."

A Great Career

For use
with Step 5:
Independent
Application
"A Great Career"
section

Davies loves her job because it keeps her on her toes. For instance, take the Water Monitor displayed in the *Lizards and Snakes* exhibition. What to serve this sharp-toothed lizard? In the wild, it uses its forked tongue to "smell" its prey—live rats. But the museum isn't in the business of raising packs of rats, so when it came to mealtime, more imaginative strategies were needed. Davies had to dangle a dead rat from the tip of long tongs so the 1-meter (3-foot) long lizard could sniff it out. "Every morning, I would find the lizard waiting at the door for me—almost like a dog," she says.

And then there was the time when she brought a breakfast of crickets to a 30-centimeter (1-foot) long lizard that climbs and clings to trees with gripping toe pads. The lizard—a leaftailed gecko—leapt into the air and landed on her face. "I thought it was asleep," says Davies. "It was funny, but after that I was more aware of where it was every time I opened the cage."

Right There/Think & Search QARs

GOAL • Introduce the two types of In the Book QARs:
Right There and Think & Search

I Can Statement

I can distinguish between Right There and Think & Search QARs and use this knowledge to improve my comprehension.

Materials *(See CD for reproducibles.)*

▶ "The Secret of Gardens" by Anonymous (informational passage), p. 25
(one copy for each student)

▶ In the Book QARs Poster (display copy, one copy for each student)

▶ QAR Self-Assessment Thinksheet (one copy for each student)

BEFORE READING	DURING READING	AFTER READING

Step **1** EXPLICIT EXPLANATION

Ask students to recall the two types of QARs introduced in the previous lesson: In the Book and In My Head. Display the I Can Statement. Then tell students that in this lesson they will learn to distinguish between the two types of In the Book QARs:

▶ Right There

▶ Think & Search

Display the In the Book QARs Poster and introduce the concept:

> *Let me explain the key difference between Right There and Think & Search QARs. Sometimes, the information you need to answer a question is Right There in one place. For example, the two sentences that contain the answer are right next to one another. Other times, the information you need to answer a question is spread out, so you have to Think & Search in several different places to find it. For example, you might have to look across paragraphs, or in a chart and a paragraph, or across sections or chapters.*

Step **2** MODELING

Read the title, the nursery rhyme, and the first paragraph of the passage. If students are not familiar with the nursery rhyme, provide them with the necessary background knowledge. Then display the following questions:

▶ What are perennials? [*Right There: plants that return each year without replanting*]

▶ What are annuals? [*Right There: plants that have to be planted each year*]

▶ What is the difference between perennials and annuals? [*Think & Search: Perennials don't have to be replanted each year; annuals do*]

Now I'm going to identify the QARs to help me answer these three questions. When I look at these questions, I recognize that all the information I need to answer them is In the Book. Some answers could be Right There in one place, and some answers could require me to Think & Search across the text. (Point to the word perennials.) Right next to the word "perennials," the text says that perennials are plants that return each year without replanting. All the information I need to answer the question is Right There in the same place. (Point to the word annuals.) The same thing is true for the question about annuals. The final question is a Think & Search QAR because I have to put information together from different places; in this case, two different sentences.

Step **3** GUIDED PRACTICE

Hand out a copy of the passage to each student.

Now I want you to give it a try. Listen as I read the next section of "The Secret of Gardens." When I finish, I will ask you to use what you know about Right There and Think & Search QARs so that we can answer three more questions.

Display the following three questions:

▶ What happens when fields are plowed more often? [*Right There: topsoil loses rich nutrients every time it is plowed.*]

▶ What happened during the Great Dust Bowl? [*Right There: Poor soil conditions led to great food shortages.*]

▶ Why should farmers consider planting perennials? [*Think & Search: Students need to combine the meaning of perennial from the first paragraph with the idea that planting perennials reduces the loss of topsoil, as stated in the second paragraph.*]

Guide students to identify the QARs and answer the questions.

Step 4 COACHING

Now that you have practiced identifying Right There and Think & Search QARs with me, I want you to work with a partner to read the next section of text. Then use your understanding of Right There and Think & Search QARs to help you answer the two questions: Identify the QAR, write your answer to the question, and be prepared to share the evidence you used to answer the question.

While students work, monitor and facilitate their use of Right There and Think & Search QARs. Provide additional support as needed. Then display the following questions:

▸ What are four benefits of using perennials? [*Think & Search: Fields would not have to be tilled every year, soil could refresh its nutrients; perennials are less prone to disease; perennials come back regardless of climate changes; and farmers are able to use fewer pesticides.*]

▸ Why is it better to use fewer pesticides on farm crops? [*Right There: This approach keeps groundwater cleaner.*]

Ask students to share their answers and the corresponding QARs.

Step 5 INDEPENDENT APPLICATION

Now that you have practiced identifying In the Book QARs with a partner, I want you to try it on your own. Please read the final section of this passage independently. Then identify whether the QAR is Right There or Think & Search and answer the two questions. Be prepared to share the evidence you used. Remember, you may need to use information from the entire passage to answer these questions.

While students are reading, display the following questions:

▸ If perennials don't produce as much food as annuals, what would be the effect? [*Right There: More land would be needed to grow the same amount of food we grow now.*]

▸ What are two things scientists at The Land Institute have learned? [*Think & Search: Poor soil conditions created the Great Dust Bowl and country-wide food shortages, replacing annuals with perennials could avoid these problems.*]

Step **6** SELF-ASSESSMENT & GOAL SETTING

Prepare students to share their answers and evidence.

> *How did knowing about the two types of In the Book QARs help you in answering the questions?*

Allow several students to share their ideas. Then return their focus to the goal of the lesson in preparation for completing the QAR Self-Assessment Thinksheet. Revisit the I Can Statement:

> *I can distinguish between Right There and Think & Search QARs and use this knowledge to improve my comprehension.*

Remind students that understanding In the Book QARs can support their understanding of text and the answering of questions.

> *Now, I would like you to think about how you can use this strategy in other areas and how you can add it to your own personal toolkit for reading.*

Have students complete the QAR Self-Assessment Thinksheet and turn it in with the answers to the final two questions.

The Secret of Gardens
By Anonymous

For use with
Step 2: Modeling

title, nursery
rhyme, and first
2 paragraphs

How does your garden grow?

With silver bells and cockle shells and pretty maids all in a row.

Farms across the United States produce enough food to feed our country, as well as enough food to send aid around the world. But do these professional growers have something to learn from Mary and her little flower garden? The Land Institute in Salina, Kansas, thinks so.

Mary's "silver bells" and "cockle shells" are flowers that are called perennials, which means that they return each year, without replanting. Annuals are plants that must be replanted before each growing season. Crops like corn and wheat are annuals, but scientists believe that have found a way to create corn and wheat perennials.

Why do it?

For use with
Step 3: Guided
Practice

"Why do it?"
heading and
first paragraph

As the world's population has grown, fields need to be plowed more often, losing a little more nutrient-rich topsoil each time. Scientists at The Land Institute know that in the United States during the 1930s, poor soil conditions created the Great Dust Bowl, and led to countrywide food shortages. They are concerned that although the great volume of food that farms produce is necessary, their methods may be dangerous.

For use with
Step 4: Coaching

"Why do it?"
second
paragraph

Replacing annuals with perennials means that fields would not have to be tilled every year and the soil would have a chance to refresh its nutrients. As every dandelion proves, perennials are tougher than annuals. Because they are less prone to disease, perennials come back year after year, regardless of most climate changes. This means that farmers would be able to use fewer pesticides which would keep groundwater cleaner.

For use
with Step 5:
Independent
Application

"Why do it?"
third paragraph

This technology is not perfect yet. Some people believe that perennials might not produce as much corn or wheat as annuals, which would mean that more land would be needed for farming. The Land Institute believes that the higher-nutrient level in the soil will fix this, but only time and research will tell. The other large question is one for you—if you could choose bread and cereal that were made with perennial wheat instead of annual wheat, would you?

Author & Me/On My Own QARs

GOAL ● Introduce the two types of In My Head Book QARs: Author & Me and On My Own

I Can Statement

I can distinguish between Author & Me and On My Own QARs and use this knowledge to improve my comprehension.

Materials *(See CD for reproducibles.)*

▶ "Surprises" by Michael Priestley (narrative passage), p. 30 (one copy for each student)

▶ In My Head QARs Poster (display copy)

▶ QAR Self-Assessment Thinksheet (one copy for each student)

BEFORE READING   DURING READING   AFTER READING

Step 1 EXPLICIT EXPLANATION

Remind students of the two types of QARs introduced in Lesson 1—In the Book and In My Head—and that they have already learned about the two kinds of In the Book QARs: Right There and Think & Search. Tell them that in this lesson they will learn about the two kinds of In My Head QARs: Author & Me and On My Own.

Display the In My Head QARs poster.

> *Today we are going to learn about the two types of In My Head QARs. Sometimes when an answer is found In My Head, I have to use the clues the author gives me and my own knowledge to answer the question—this is called Author & Me. Other times I can simply rely on my own prior knowledge. We call that type of QAR, On My Own.*

Step 2 MODELING

Display the passage and read the title and the first three paragraphs. As you read aloud, occasionally pause and think aloud to share your thoughts about the text with students. Then display the following questions:

▸ Why did Lin's mother put the canary next to Lin's bed while he slept? [*Author & Me: She wanted to surprise Lin with his birthday present when he woke up.*]

▸ What is the biggest birthday surprise you have ever received? [*On My Own: Answers will vary depending upon students' experiences.*]

▸ What do you think will happen to Lin's canary? [*Author & Me: Predictions will vary but students should be able to justify them.*]

Now that I have read the text, I'm going to identify the QARs to help me answer these three questions. The author has given me several clues to answer the first question but doesn't really give me the information I need, so this is an Author & Me QAR. I will use the author clues to decide on the best information In My Head to answer the question. Since Lin's mother wants to surprise him on his birthday, I think she will put his present by the bed while Lin is sleeping so that he'll be surprised when he wakes up. Question 2 is one I can answer On My Own without even reading the story. My biggest birthday surprise was [describe a surprise]. The third question asks me to make a prediction, so I will need to use the author's clues and information In My Head. The text states that Lin thought of the bird as a prisoner in its cage, that the bird likes to flutter around its cage, and that Lin lifted the canary from its cage. I know from the information In My Head that birds can easily fly away, get lost, and not be able to return home, so that is what I predict will happen.

Step 3 GUIDED PRACTICE

Now I want you to give it a try. Listen as I read the next section of "Surprises." Then I will ask you to use what you know about the two In My Head QARs—Author & Me and On My Own—to answer three more questions.

You may want to distribute copies of the passage to students so they can follow along as you read. After you read the next paragraph aloud, display the following questions:

▸ Have you ever lost something that meant a lot to you? What happened? [*On My Own: Answers will vary based on students' background experiences.*]

▸ How do you think Lin's mom felt? [*Author & Me: Clues that she may have felt responsible or felt guilty include she was the one who had opened the door and let the canary escape, she had no way of knowing Lin had let the canary out, she sat with Lin outside for over an hour to no avail. Students should justify their answers.*]

Step 4 COACHING

If you have not yet passed out copies of the text, do so now.

> *Now that you have practiced using Author & Me and On My Own QARs with me to improve comprehension, I want you to work with a partner to read the next section of text. Then use your knowledge of these QARs to create your best answer to each question. If you decide that the QAR is Author & Me, you know that you need to rely on the text to point you to useful In My Head background knowledge and experiences. If you decide that the QAR is On My Own, you know that you don't need to rely on the text and can just start with your own background knowledge and experiences.*

While students work, monitor and facilitate their use of Author & Me and On My Own QARs. Provide additional support as needed. When some students begin to finish the reading, display the following questions:

> ▶ What else could Lin have done to find his canary? [*Author & Me: Students need to know what Lin had already done (information provided by the author) before suggesting alternatives such as posting signs, getting neighbors to help look, leaving out food.*]

> ▶ Why do people throw pennies into fountains? [*On My Own: Answers will vary depending on students' cultural knowledge and background experiences with wishing wells.*]

Have several students share the QAR they selected and their answers. Point out that thinking about the QAR—whether Author & Me or On My Own—helps readers know the sources of information they should use to answer a question.

Step 5 INDEPENDENT APPLICATION

> *Now that you have practiced identifying In My Head QARs with a partner, I want you to try it independently. Please read the final section of the passage on your own. Then identify the QAR—whether Author & Me or On My Own— and answer the questions. For each question, identify the QAR, answer the question, and be prepared to share the information you used.*

While students are reading, display the following questions:

> ▶ What would you write if you were asked to describe an amazing event in your life? [*On My Own: Answers will vary depending on students' interests and what they consider to be the most amazing event in their lives.*]

▶ Which event in this story did you find the most surprising and why? [*Author & Me: Answers will vary but could include Lin receiving the canary as a birthday gift, the canary flying away, or the canary becoming Renda's pet.*]

Step 6 SELF-ASSESSMENT & GOAL SETTING

Allow students time to complete the reading, identify the QARs, answer the questions, and prepare to share their answers and evidence. Have a few students share their work. Then lead a discussion of the following question:

How did knowing about Author & Me and On My Own—the two In My Head QARs—help you answer the questions?

Ask students to turn to a partner and discuss the question together. Then call on several pairs to share their ideas. Then return their focus to the goal of the lesson in preparation for completing their QAR Self-Assessment Thinksheet. Revisit the I Can Statement.

I can distinguish between Author & Me and On My Own QARs and use this knowledge to improve my comprehension.

Remind students that understanding these two In My Head QARs can support their understanding of text and answering of questions.

Now I would like you to think about how you can use this strategy in other areas and how you can add it to your own personal toolkit for reading.

Have students complete the QAR Self-Assessment Thinksheet and turn it in with their work on the QARs and answers for the final two questions.

Surprises

by Michael Priestley

For use with Step 2: Modeling
title and first 3 paragraphs

For just a few days when he was ten years old, Lin Peng had a pet canary. The lovely yellow bird was a birthday surprise from his mother. She brought the canary into Lin's room on the night before his birthday. While he was sleeping, she placed it on his night table. When Lin woke the next morning, he saw a box-shaped object draped with a blue silk scarf. Lin yanked away the scarf to see what it concealed. The canary, which was a bit startled, chirped and fluttered its wings. Lin gasped with delight.

Lin's mother had chosen the perfect gift. The canary fascinated Lin. He spent hours watching it flit about its cage. He borrowed *Your Pet Canary* from the library and read every page. He fed his pet the finest bird food. He gave it fresh water twice each day. The canary rewarded Lin by singing its beautiful song. Lin was sure he would never grow tired of it.

Still, one thing troubled Lin about the canary. He couldn't help thinking of it as a prisoner in its cage. He saw how much it loved to flutter from perch to perch. The canary would be even happier, Lin decided, if it could fly around inside the house. So one day while his mother was out shopping, Lin lifted the canary from its cage. He put it on his shoulder. "Go ahead," he said encouragingly. "Spread your wings and fly."

For use with Step 3: Guided Practice
next 4 paragraphs

The canary sat for a moment and looked around. Then it took off, flying from Lin's shoulder to the sofa and then to a lampshade. After resting there briefly, the canary took off down the hallway toward the kitchen. Lin laughed as he followed. He got to the kitchen just in time to see his mother, her arms filled with grocery bags, struggling to get through the open door.

Lin rushed forward to grab the bags from his mother. "Quick, Mom! Shut the door! Don't let the bird out!" he shouted. But it was too late. The canary flew over their heads and sailed outside. It landed in a bush just a few steps from the door.

As slowly and calmly as he could, Lin crept out the door toward the bush. He reached out with his hands. "Come on, little birdie, come back inside with us," Lin murmured softly.

The canary was almost within his grasp. Then it suddenly soared up high into the hemlock tree and vanished among its feathery branches. Mom soon followed Lin outside, and the two of them stood beneath the tree, hoping to spot the canary. But after almost an hour, they gave up and went inside.

For use with Step 4: Coaching
next 2 paragraphs

For the next few weeks, Lin kept searching for the canary. Each day after school, he walked around his neighborhood. He scanned the sky, the trees, and the ground, looking for a flash of yellow.

At last the day came when Lin admitted to himself that the bird was gone forever. So he dumped out his piggy bank. He filled his pockets with pennies and set off for the town square on his bike. There he tossed his pennies, one by one, into a fountain. With each toss, he made a wish. He wished aloud that his dear canary had found a good home.

For use with Step 5: Independent Application
remainder of story

Two years passed. The guilt that Lin felt about losing the canary slowly faded away. In fact, he had almost forgotten about the canary. Then came the day in class when Renda Masud stirred his memories.

In class that day, Ms. Paloma had asked the students to write an essay. It was supposed to tell about an amazing event in their lives. Most of the students had to ponder the topic before they started writing, but Renda began immediately. When it was time for the students to read their essays aloud, Ms. Paloma called on Renda first.

"Two years ago," Renda began, "the most amazing thing happened to me. I was sitting on our back porch reading a book. Suddenly, out of nowhere, a beautiful canary appeared. It settled on the porch railing. I watched it for a few moments. Then I got up slowly and opened the door to the house. The canary flew inside. That's how Goldie became my pet."

Lin's jaw dropped open. He could hardly believe what he was hearing. Then he thought back to the fountain in the town square. Lin remembered the pennies he had tossed into the water. And he realized that his wish had come true.

QAR and the Reading Cycle

GOAL ● Teach students about QARs and the reading cycle

I Can Statement

I can use QARs to improve my comprehension throughout the reading cycle: before reading, during reading, and after reading.

Materials *(See CD for reproducibles.)*

▶ "Out of This World" by Mona Chiang (informational passage), p. 36 (one copy for each student)

▶ Core QARs Poster (display copy)

▶ QAR and the Reading Cycle Poster (display copy)

▶ QAR Self-Assessment Thinksheet (one copy for each student)

Step **1** EXPLICIT EXPLANATION

Today's lesson focuses on the reading cycle (before, during, and after reading) and is designed to help students understand how to apply QARs during each part of the cycle. Display the I Can Statement and the QAR and the Reading Cycle Poster. Begin by explaining the reading cycle to students.

> *Today we are going to learn about the three parts of the reading cycle and how QARs can help you comprehend what you read throughout the cycle. As a reader, you have already experienced the entire reading cycle, although you may not have called it that. We call the first part of the reading cycle "before reading." There are some things you do before you begin to read, such as thinking of what you already know about the topic, the author, or genre. We call the second part of the reading cycle "during reading." There are some things you do while you are reading the text, such as thinking about important ideas or how ideas connect to one another. We call the third part of the reading cycle "after reading." There are some things you do when you have finished reading the text, such as thinking about the author's message or theme, new information you've learned, or how the text could help you in your life.*

Now help students see the connection between the reading cycle and QARs.

Certain QARs are more common before, during, or after reading. Knowing which type of QAR you are likely to find in each part of the reading cycle can guide you to make the best use of information both In My Head and In the Book. Active readers are always asking and answering questions as they move through the reading cycle, and knowing about QARs can help with these questions.

Use the Core QARs Poster to review the four different QARs.

Step **2** MODELING

BEFORE READING   DURING READING   AFTER READING

Tell students that good readers use their knowledge of QARs to generate useful questions and respond to the questions posed by others before, during, and after reading. Display the passage's title and illustration along with the following question:

▶ What do the illustration and the title, "Out of this World," suggest this text might be about? [*On My Own: Answers will vary based on students' background knowledge but could include a focus on space travel or the genre of nonfiction.*]

Let's start by thinking about QARs that often occur before reading, which is the first part of the reading cycle. Before reading, I usually look at the title and opening illustration and think about what I know about the general topic of the text. I ask myself what the text might be about, based on just the title or pictures. If I am going to introduce a text to someone else, like all of you, I ask questions that will help you think about your own background knowledge or learn from each other's responses. The question you see is one that I might ask myself, or one that I might ask you, before reading.

Have students read the question aloud with you. Then discuss the QAR for this question (On My Own) and possible answers. Conclude by making sure students understand that On My Own QARs are by far the most common before reading.

Note:
We are defining On My Own QARs as those that occur when students have only minimal information about the text: title, opening illustration, author's name, and genre. On My Own QARs are those designed to help readers access relevant background knowledge, or to build knowledge from listening to others' responses if there is a group discussion before reading. Author & Me QARs that occur before reading require readers to use the text clues for action, such as when they make a specific prediction about the text (see Lessons 5 and 6).

Step **3** GUIDED PRACTICE/COACHING

DURING READING

> *Now we're ready for the second part of the reading cycle: during reading. During reading, I'm immersing myself in the world of the text. I think about the important ideas, I put these important ideas together, and I monitor my comprehension to make sure everything is making sense. The QARs most valuable during reading are Right There, Think & Search, and Author & Me. Right There QARs are useful for helping me think about what's important in the text. Think & Search QARs help me make connections among text ideas. Author & Me QARs help me draw inferences and monitor my understanding.*

Distribute a copy of the passage to each student and display the following questions:

▸ What things in Mae Jemison's childhood indicated she would become a scientist? [*Think & Search: told her kindergarten teacher she would become a scientist, loved learning—especially about the earth, liked the idea of exploring space from watching* Star Trek]

▸ How did Nichelle Nichols influence Mae Jemison, even though they never met? [*Think & Search: modeled that an African American woman could be a space explorer and scientist*]

▸ Where did Jemison work following graduation from medical school? [*Right There: Sierra Leone and Liberia in West Africa*]

▸ What do Jemison's choices for career and work tell you about the kind of person she is? [*Author & Me: Clues show that she chose to help people and continue learning, that she likes adventure.*]

Tell students that these four questions represent the kinds of questions active readers may ask themselves during reading.

> *Notice that during-reading QARs differ from before reading QARs. During-reading QARs help readers understand the text by focusing on important ideas in the text, putting those ideas together, and making relevant inferences. When I read these during-reading questions, I notice that none is likely to be an On My Own QAR. I have to look In the Book for information to answer them. Some look like the QAR might be a Right There or Think & Search QAR, where everything I need to answer the question is in one or several places. But some might be Author & Me QARs, where I will use clues from the text to help me decide what information In My Head will be most useful.*

Read the text with the students. Then discuss each question in terms of the QAR, the information that was used to answer the question, and the evidence that supports the choice of QAR. Promote the gradual release of responsibility to students as follows:

- **Question 1:** Read the question, identify the QAR, use the QAR to model the search for appropriate information to answer the question, and provide evidence to support the choice of QAR and the answer.

- **Question 2:** Read the question, identify the QAR, and use it to model the information search. Ask students to provide evidence to support the choice of QAR and answer.

- **Question 3:** Read the question and identify the QAR. Ask students to search for appropriate information and provide evidence to confirm the QAR and answer.

- **Question 4:** Read the question. Ask students to provide the QAR, answer, and evidence to justify the QAR and answer.

Write down the QAR next to each question. Ask students to describe any patterns they see. Use this opportunity to evaluate students' ability to explain the connections they now understand between QARs and the reading cycle: QARs that occur during reading are primarily Think & Search but may also be Right There or Author & Me, and that it is unusual to ask or be asked On My Own questions during reading.

Step **4** INDEPENDENT APPLICATION

DURING READING

Now that you are getting good at using what you know about QARs and the reading cycle to answer questions before, during, and after reading, I want you to work on your own.

Display the following four questions:

- What is important about the velocity of the space shuttle? [*Right There: It's fast enough to offset the pull of gravity.*]

- When Jemison was in the space shuttle flying around Earth, why was she able to do ten spins as she danced, even though she could never do that on earth? [*Think & Search: The space shuttle has a different gravity than Earth, a microgravity that is caused by the speed of the shuttle and the tug of Earth's gravity. The combination allows astronauts to float in the lower gravity. Thus, spinning ten times is possible because nothing is pulling Jemison to the floor of the spaceship.*]

- What research and projects has Jemison led aboard the shuttle and back on Earth? [*Think & Search: studying bone growth, using technology design to improve human lives, starting an international space camp, appearing on TV*]

▶ Why was it particularly important for Jemison to exercise while in space? [*Author & Me: The lower gravity in space meant that Jemison was not carrying her body weight, which would have allowed her bones to weaken. By exercising, she put weight or stress on her muscles and bones, keeping them strong.*]

Read the rest of the text with these questions in mind. Look at the questions and think about the QAR and source of the information you will likely need for answering each one. As you read, use your knowledge of QAR to create excellent answers to each question. Be prepared to share your thinking when everyone has finished reading this section.

Step **5** SELF-ASSESSMENT & GOAL SETTING

BEFORE READING　　　DURING READING　　**AFTER READING**

Have a few students share their responses to reinforce the types of QARs that are generally found during reading: Right There, Think & Search, Author & Me. Inform students that they have now come to the third and final part of the reading cycle: after reading. Let them know that after reading, active readers often think about how the text they just read connects to their own lives. Then display the final question:

▶ From reading about Mae Jemison's life, what have you learned about your own ambitions and how to achieve them? [*Author & Me: Clues from the text include her commitment to high goals, hard work, willingness to try new things, wide variety of interests.*]

Have students identify the QAR that they used to answer the question (Author & Me). Then, ask them to turn to a partner to discuss their thoughts. Ask two or three students to share with the whole class. Elicit the idea that Author & Me QARs allow readers to use the text as a springboard for thinking about their own lives, while keeping important ideas in the text in mind. Explain that good readers often reflect on the significance of what they have read to their own lives. Indicate that for high levels of comprehension, Author & Me is the most important QAR for after reading, the final part of the reading cycle.

Ask students to complete and hand in a QAR Self-Assessment Thinksheet.

Note:
Author & Me is critical for deeper comprehension of text. It requires close reading, unlike On My Own, and, in contrast to Right There or Think & Search, it moves students to reflect upon the significance of the text.

Out of This World

By Mona Chiang

For use with
Step 2: Modeling
title and first
paragraph

Mae Jemison looked out the window and saw Chicago passing by. The scientist wasn't looking out of any old window. She was observing her childhood hometown from far above Earth's surface—from the space shuttle.

In 1987, Jemison was selected to become an astronaut, making her the first African-American female astronaut. In 1992, she made world history as the first woman of color in space. As the science mission specialist onboard *Endeavor*, she performed experiments while the shuttle made 127 orbits at roughly 482 kilometers (260 nautical miles) above Earth. "Each day was exciting and challenging," says Jemison of her experience in space.

For use with
Step 3: Guided
Practice/Coaching
next 2 paragraphs
and "Aim High"
section

In some ways, Jemison's trip into space had been in her plans even before she completed kindergarten. One day, the 5-year-old boldly announced to her teacher that she planned to be a scientist.

Aim High

As a child, Jemison's curiosity about the world sent her on frequent trips to the library. There, she devoured books on many different subjects. In fourth grade, "I particularly loved learning about how Earth was created," she says. "I wanted to know how life evolved, how we ended up here, and how big space was."

The budding scientist also enjoyed watching the 1960s TV show *Star Trek*. She found the character Lieutenant Uhura particularly engaging. Played by African-American actress Nichelle Nichols, the chief communications officer explored the galaxy with a crew made up of people from all over the world. This vision fueled Jemison's belief that she, too, would explore space.

At age 16, Jemison entered Stanford University in California, where she earned degrees in chemical engineering and African Studies. She continued her studies by going to medical school at Cornell University in New York City and becoming a physician.

Following medical school, Jemison worked as the Area Peace Corps Medical Officer for Sierra Leone and Liberia in West Africa, bringing health care to people in those nations. She also worked as a general practitioner in Los Angeles, California. While working there, she applied for a spot with NASA. In 1987, she was selected to become an astronaut.

For use
with Step 4:
Independent
Application
"Blast Off"
section

Blast Off

On September 12, 1992, Jemison lifted off from Earth and spent eight days working aboard *Endeavour*. "It feels very different from being on Earth," she says of living in space.

Aboard the shuttle, astronauts float because they experience gravity a little differently than they do on Earth. This attracting force that pulls objects toward one another is everywhere, even in space. You are pulled to Earth's surface because Earth is so massive. To avoid being dragged back to Earth's surface, the space shuttle travels very quickly around Earth—at speeds of approximately 28,000 km (17,500 mi) per hour. That velocity (speed in one direction) is just fast enough to offset the pull of gravity. The shuttle's forward velocity combines with the downward pull of Earth's gravity, bending the path of the shuttle as it falls. So instead of falling directly down to Earth, the space shuttle and its astronauts fall in a path around Earth. Since the shuttle and the astronauts inside are falling together at the same rate, the astronauts float.

Jemison, an avid dancer, tried dancing in this microgravity environment. "It felt very free," she says. "For example, I could easily spin 10 times around, which I can't do here on Earth." While moving in weightlessness is fun, the microgravity environment can be harsh on the body. "Your muscles start to weaken because you're not carrying your body weight," says Jemison. Also, when no stress is placed on the bones, the bones weaken. One of Jemison's onboard experiments studied bone growth in microgravity.

Jemison left NASA in 1993. Since then, she has worked in several other areas, including designing technology that could help improve human lives, teaching at universities, and starting The Earth We Share, an international space camp. She even appeared in an episode of the TV show *Star Trek: The Next Generation*.

Does Jemison think that she has accomplished everything that she wants to do in life? "Absolutely not. I'm still making up things."

Predicting With Narrative Text

GOAL • Help students understand how making predictions before and during reading can enhance comprehension

I Can Statement

I can make predictions by using the QAR Author & Me Prediction Chart.

Reading Cycle and QAR

Reading Cycle: Before and During Reading

QAR: *Author & Me:* Using author's clues to identify useful background knowledge and experiences

Materials *(See CD for reproducibles.)*

▶ "Miles to Freedom" by Elena Cabral (narrative passage), p. 43 (one copy for each student)

▶ Core QAR Poster (display copy)

▶ QARs and the Reading Cycle Poster (display copy)

(Refer to the posters as necessary during the lesson.)

▶ QAR Author & Me Prediction Chart (display copy, one copy for each pair and for each student)

▶ QAR Self-Assessment Thinksheet (one copy for each student)

BEFORE READING   DURING READING   AFTER READING

Step **1** EXPLICIT EXPLANATION

Let students know that the focus of this lesson is on prediction, an important comprehension strategy used before and during reading.

> *Today I will be teaching you about an important comprehension strategy that is used before and during reading: prediction. Before and during reading, good readers are constantly asking themselves the question, "What do I think is going to happen in this text?" The QAR is Author & Me because we need clues from the author to identify the information In My Head that can help me make reasonable predictions. I will be showing you how to use the Author & Me Prediction Chart to keep track of information In the Book, information from In My Head, and the predictions you create.*

Step 2 MODELING

Tell students that you will be using the QAR Author & Me Prediction Chart to help you make good predictions. Display the blank chart and go over the heading for each column: Author (In the Book information), Me (In My Head information), and Prediction (comprehension strategy).

> *Knowing prediction is an Author & Me QAR, basically asking the question, "What do I think will happen next?" helps me remember to use the clues the author gives me in the text to think about what I know that might help me make sense of what I am reading. Notice that the first column heading, Author, reminds me to use the author's clues. The second column heading, Me, reminds me to use my own knowledge and experiences to think about what I know that is relevant to the text. The third column, Prediction, puts the QAR together. I am working with the author to figure out what might happen next using clues in the text and information I already know.*

Once you feel students understand the connection to QAR language, model how to use the QAR Author & Me Prediction Chart to develop good predictions.

> *The title of the text we will be reading today is "Miles to Freedom." The first thing I do as a reader is to think about what the title might mean. I'm writing the title, "Miles to Freedom," in the Author column since this is what the author has written In the Book. I know that a lot of people have had to travel a long way to achieve their freedom: the slaves in America's South, refugees in Africa, prisoners of war, and even convicts who try to escape from jail. This information comes from In My Head so I'm going to write it in the Me column. (Write "Many people had to go a long way to achieve freedom" in the chart). Starting from the author's information, and using my own knowledge, I predict that the text will be about someone who had to go on a long journey to find freedom. I'll write my prediction in the chart.*

QAR Author & Me Prediction Chart

AUTHOR	ME	PREDICTION
"Miles to Freedom"	Many people had to go a long way to achieve freedom.	The text will be about someone who had to go on a long journey to find freedom.

Explain that you're going to read the first two sentences of the text aloud to see if you can confirm or add to your prediction. After reading the first two sentences aloud, model your use of text information to refine your prediction. As you speak, enter key information from the text in the Author column.

Okay, so now I know that the text is about African Americans who were enslaved in the South. I know there are two people in the story, and they are living in Georgia when the story begins.

Continue modeling and enter information in the Me column.

I know that many slaves escaped from the South to the North using the Underground Railroad.

Finish modeling by entering information in the Prediction column of the chart.

Using these clues from the author, I can make a more specific prediction: Ellen and William will leave Georgia to escape slavery. I think they will travel for a long distance before they actually get to freedom. I wonder if they will use the Underground Railroad on their journey.

AUTHOR	ME	PREDICTION
African Americans, enslaved in the South, two people, living in Georgia	Underground Railroad	Ellen and William will leave Georgia to escape slavery. They will travel for a long distance.

DURING READING

Step 3 GUIDED PRACTICE

Tell students that now they'll practice using the QAR Author & Me Prediction Chart for making and refining predictions, following the same steps you just modeled. Display the passage.

I'm going to read the next section of text to you. While I read, I want you to help me think about the information that can be added to each column in the chart: clues from the author, our own background knowledge, and possible predictions.

Use your own ideas, as well as your students' ideas, for this portion of the text. The sample below will help you get started.

Note:
Seek to move students away from focusing on getting the right answer to thinking in a logical manner. Be sure to praise students who show logical thinking, even if their predictions do not turn out to be accurate.

AUTHOR	ME	PREDICTION
Ellen had light skin.	Some black people's light-tone skin looks the same as white people's skin.	Ellen might be able to escape because people will think she's white.

Step 4 COACHING

Hand out copies of the passage to students. Have them draw their own QAR Author & Me Prediction Chart on a sheet of notebook paper.

> *Work with a partner to read the next section of this story. You should take turns reading the text to each other and then make at least three new predictions. Remember that you are asking yourself, "What do I think is going to happen in this text?" The QAR for this question is Author & Me, and this reminds you to use what the author has written to help you identify useful In My Head information. I will be circulating to observe your thinking.*

As you circulate to observe your students' thinking, encourage anyone who finishes early to add more Author-Me-Prediction entries to their charts. You can also ask them to add their entries to the class chart you began earlier. A sample chart entry for this portion of the text appears below.

AUTHOR	ME	PREDICTION
Ellen bandaged her head and arm and would tell people she was headed north for medical treatment.	When people plan disguises, they have to be organized and prepared so they don't get caught in a lie.	Ellen might forget her story or use her hand. Then she and William would be caught.

Step 5 INDEPENDENT APPLICATION

> *Read the rest of the story on your own. As you read, keep asking yourself, "What do I think is going to happen in this text?" Add at least three new predictions to your chart.*

As before, encourage students who finish early to add more Author-Me-Prediction entries to their charts. Invite a few students to add their entries to the class chart. Then call the whole group back together and ask some students to share entries from their charts. A sample chart entry for the final portion of the text appears below.

AUTHOR	ME	PREDICTION
"But she quickly steadied herself."	In a dangerous situation, it is easy to panic and make mistakes.	Ellen will be able to escape because she knows how to remain calm when faced with a dangerous situation.

As students share, guide them to the understanding that using clues In the Book to identify useful information In My Head can lead them to make sound predictions.

Step **6** SELF-ASSESSMENT & GOAL SETTING

Display the I Can Statement.

> *The purpose of this lesson was to help you learn to use predictions before and during reading to improve your comprehension of the text. We learned to make predictions by using the QAR Author & Me Prediction Chart.*

Call on volunteers to explain how they used the QAR Author & Me Prediction Chart to make predictions.

> *Now I would like you to think about how you can use the strategy of prediction in other areas and how you can add prediction to your own personal toolkit for reading.*

Then have students complete a QAR Self-Assessment Thinksheet and turn it in with their chart.

Miles to Freedom

By Elena Cabral

For use with
Step 2: Modeling
title and first
paragraph

William and Ellen Craft met in Macon, Georgia, in the 1840s. Like other African-Americans in the antebellum (pre-Civil War) South, they lived under the harsh conditions of slavery.

Ellen was the daughter of a white lawyer and his black slave. In the South, her mixed blood and light skin afforded her no special treatment. She was separated from her mother and sold to another family.

For use with
Step 3: Guided
Practice
next
2 paragraphs

Although William and Ellen lived as slaves, they were allowed to marry. While working for a white family in Macon, they decided to risk their lives for freedom.

In the months before Christmas of 1848, the Crafts planned their escape. Ellen, who was then 22, would disguise herself as a white man. William, her 24-year-old husband, would pose as her slave.

For use with
Step 4: Coaching
next
4 paragraphs

Since no white woman would travel with a male slave, Ellen had to pretend that she was a man. She would say that she needed medical treatment up North. The Crafts decided to travel to Philadelphia, in the free state of Pennsylvania.

It was a dangerous plan. If caught, the husband and wife could be beaten or killed, and would surely be separated forever.

"A Desperate Leap"

To help disguise Ellen, William bought her dark green eyeglasses and a tall beaver hat. She sewed herself a pair of men's trousers and wrapped a bandage around her head to hide her soft, beardless face.

For use
with Step 5:
Independent
Application
remainder of
passage

But there was a problem. William and Ellen were illiterate, because it was illegal for anyone to teach a slave to read. What if someone asked Ellen to sign a hotel register or other document? This could put her in grave danger. To avoid having to write, Ellen would wear a sling on her arm.

Just days before Christmas, William cut Ellen's long hair. They were finally ready to leave, having gotten a special pass from their owners for the holiday. No one knew that they did not plan to return.

The morning of their departure, William opened the door to their cabin and whispered to his wife. "Come, my dear," he said. "Let us make a desperate leap for liberty."

At first, Ellen shrank back in sobs, overwhelmed by the dangers they were about to face. But she quickly steadied herself.

The journey almost ended before it began. A white man who had known Ellen her whole life sat beside her on a train to Savannah, Georgia.

"It is a very fine morning, sir, isn't it?" the man said to Ellen. Would she be discovered if she answered?

Ellen hoped that the man would think she was deaf. Finally, she decided to answer his questions, softly and briefly. He didn't suspect a thing.

The couple traveled by train and steamer (ship), facing one close call after another.

When Ellen was asked to sign a document proving that William was her slave, another passenger came forward to help her.

But there was one more obstacle. On Christmas Eve, as they boarded the train for the final leg of their journey—from Baltimore, Maryland, to Philadelphia—a railroad officer stopped William.

"Where are you going?"

"To Philadelphia, sir," William replied. "I'm with my master."

"You have to get approval first."

William and Ellen were terrified. Then Ellen had an idea. Rather than show fear, she would demand respect, something a slave could never do.

"I bought tickets all the way to Philadelphia," she said angrily. "You have no right to detain [hold back or keep] us!" At that moment, the train's whistle blew. The officer gave up, and the Crafts took their seats.

It was Christmas Day when they finally arrived in Philadelphia.

"Thank God," Ellen exclaimed. "We are safe!"

The Crafts' story did not end there. They joined an abolitionist movement and gave speeches about their escape. Slave catchers began to pursue them everywhere.

Under the fugitive slave laws, if the Crafts were caught, they could be returned to the family in Georgia that still claimed them as their property. So the couple fled to England.

After the Civil War ended, in 1865, they returned to Georgia to help former slaves. They became known everywhere for their daring escape.

Predicting With Informational Text

GOAL • Help students understand how making predictions can enhance comprehension by focusing their attention as they read

I Can Statement

I can make predictions about texts before and during reading, using Author & Me QARs, so I know how to focus my attention when I read.

Reading Cycle & QAR

Reading Cycle: Before and During Reading

QAR: *Author & Me:* Using author's clues to identify useful background knowledge and experiences

Materials *(See CD for reproducibles.)*

▶ "A Real-Life Spider-Man" by Barry Rust (informational passage), p. 50 (one copy for each student)

▶ Core QARs Poster (display copy)

▶ QAR and the Reading Cycle Poster (display copy)

(Refer to the posters as necessary during the lesson.)

▶ QAR Author & Me T-Chart (display copy, one copy for each pair and for each student)

▶ QAR Self-Assessment Thinksheet (one copy for each student)

| BEFORE READING | DURING READING | AFTER READING |

Step 1 EXPLICIT EXPLANATION

Tell students that the purpose of today's lesson is to learn to determine how accurate your predictions have been. Remind them that they will need to draw on clues from the author and use their own knowledge to see if your predictions have been supported. Review what students learned in Lesson 5, eliciting two key ideas. First, predictions are Author & Me QARs that explore the implicit question, "What do I think will happen next in the text I am reading?" Second, the column headings in the QAR Author & Me Prediction Chart are Author, Me, and Predictions. This is a reminder to start with the text and use the information in it to identify useful knowledge and experiences In My Head, and then make a prediction. End by explaining what happens when a prediction turns out to be inaccurate:

Good readers promote their comprehension by making predictions before and during reading. When I read, I use clues from the author to think about how accurate my predictions have been. Does information in the text support— or fail to support—my predictions? If my predictions aren't supported, then I must think about what else I know that might make sense.

Step **2** MODELING

Tell students that because they have done well with making predictions, they will now be testing the predictions they create. You are going to introduce a new tool, the QAR Author & Me T-Chart, which will help them organize text clues that they will use to test their predictions. Display the QAR Author & Me T-Chart.

QAR Author & Me T-Chart

PREDICTIONS	TEXT EVIDENCE

Predicting helps focus my attention during reading because I can read to see if the author's words support, or fail to support, my predictions. If one of my predictions isn't supported, I know I should call on more background knowledge and revise my thinking. This QAR Author & Me T-Chart is another useful tool I can use when making predictions. This chart can help me organize the evidence in the text that lets me know whether my prediction is supported.

Display "A Real-Life Spider-Man." Explain that you will write your predictions about this passage in the first column, adding notes from the text in the second column. Let students know that you will be checking your predictions for accuracy and modifying your thinking as necessary.

To create my first prediction, I'll start by looking at the author's first clue, the title, "A Real-Life Spider-Man." Given the idea of "real life" and Spider-Man, I now am thinking about what I know. "Real-life" makes me think this is someone who really exists. "Spider-Man" makes me think of the superhero.

And spiders make me think of making threads and webs. I actually have
two possible predictions. My first prediction is that the text might be about a
superhero like Spider-Man—but about a real man who does heroic things.

Write this first prediction in the first column of the T-chart [about a real man who
does heroic things].

My second prediction is that the text might be about someone who works
with spiders.

Write this second prediction beneath the first prediction [about someone who works
with spiders].

Explain that when you read, you will be looking for clues in the text that either
support or fail to support your predictions. Checking your predictions is a good way to
make sure that the text is making sense to you and to find out if you need to rethink
your ideas.

Read the first paragraph aloud and have students follow along on the displayed copy.
As you read aloud, jot down information in the Text Evidence column on the right-
hand side of the T-chart. That information may include: movie set, spider is tiny star
of scene, *Steatoda grossa* spider, appears on cue.

The author's clues help me test my prediction. One idea makes me think
my prediction that Spider-Man is a superhero is accurate, because they are on a
movie set. But I don't think that fits the title, a "real-life" superhero. The ideas
that a spider appears on cue as a tiny star in the movie, and that we are told
the scientific name of the spider, make me think my second prediction may be
closer. However, I think I need to modify that prediction. My new prediction is
that it's about someone who knows how to train spiders, and the next section
is going to tell us how he does this job.

Add this new prediction to the T-Chart.

Step 3 GUIDED PRACTICE

Read the next section of the passage with students. Give them the opportunity
to identify text evidence related to the predictions as you read. Record the text
information students provide in the Text Evidence column of the QAR Author & Me
T-Chart, such as bug scientist, coaches insects so they will behave in certain ways in
films, creates environments so they are likely to react in a certain way.

Return to the three predictions. Lead students to discuss each prediction, identifying
the text evidence that indicated it was accurate or inaccurate. Tell students that you
may cross out the inaccurate predictions, and model this action by crossing out the
first prediction.

Step 4 COACHING

Provide each student with a copy of the passage. Have partners work together to read and make predictions about the next paragraph. Before they begin, ask each to draw his or her own QAR Author & Me T-Chart on a piece of notebook paper. Then tell students to write down predictions for the next section of text and jot down the clues in the text that help support, reject, or refine those predictions.

Allow students time to work and circulate around the class to provide assistance as needed. When students are finished, ask several pairs to share their predictions and text clues that support or fail to support their predictions. Record students' ideas in the appropriate columns of the class QAR Author & Me T-Chart. Discuss how some predictions were supported by text evidence, while others were not. See if any students wrote and then crossed out a prediction. Ask those students to share examples of predictions they decided to refine.

Step 5 INDEPENDENT APPLICATION

Explain to students that they will now be making and checking predictions on their own, using the individual QAR Author & Me T-Chart they started earlier.

Make your final predictions for the remainder of the text. Then use the author's clues to find out whether or not your prediction is supported.

Then ask for volunteers to share their predictions, relevant information from the author, and whether their predictions were supported by the text. Encourage students to discuss the information from the author that supported, or failed to support, their predictions.

AFTER READING

Step 6 SELF-ASSESSMENT & GOAL SETTING

Display the I Can Statement and ask students to keep it in mind as they think about what they have learned.

I can make predictions about texts before and during reading, using Author & Me QARs, so I know how to focus my attention when I read.

Then ask students to talk with a partner about what they learned about creating and testing predictions, and how that helped them understand the text. Elicit several student responses, such as how the QAR Author & Me T-Chart helped them test their predictions, set a focus for reading, and read carefully to see if their predictions were supported. Point out that active readers use this kind of thinking to make sense of what they are reading.

Remind students that predictions will vary among readers and that the goal is not to find the right prediction, but rather to use their predictions to help them understand the texts they read.

Think about how you can use this strategy in other areas and how you can add this to your personal toolkit for reading.

Tell students to complete the QAR Self-Assessment Thinksheet and turn it in with their QAR Author & Me T-Chart.

A Real-Life Spider-Man

By Barry Rust

For use with Step 2: Modeling
title and first paragraph

The set of the movie *Spider-Man* is buzzing with activity. Set designers slide the last props into place; hairdressers squirt hair products on Tobey Maguire and Kirsten Dunst as they step onto their marks. "Quiet on the set!" an assistant shouts. Finally, the director yells "Action!" The actors bustle through the scene, but the camera is focused on the smallest star in the entire movie—a tiny *Steatoda grossa* spider. Right on cue, it descends from the ceiling on a thread of webbing.

For use with Step 3: Guided Practice
next 2 paragraphs

The director is thrilled. Just off camera, a bearded bug scientist smiles, holding a case full of the Steatoda grossa spiders. His name is Steve Kutcher, and in Hollywood, he's a real-life spider-man. His job is to coax spiders, cockroaches, mealworms, wasps, and all kinds of other insects to be movie stars in films like *Jurassic Park* and *James and the Giant Peach*.

Kutcher doesn't teach a bug to fetch or roll over on command like a dog trainer. Instead, he creates environments to make bugs react a certain way. Right before shooting the scene in *Spider-Man*, Kutcher picked a spider that looked ready to web down. Since Steatoda grossa spiders are most likely to web down in the evening, he asked the director to shoot the scene at that time of day.

For use with Step 4: Coaching
next paragraph

"There's no guidebook for this," Kutcher explains. "I just use my knowledge and expertise." Kutcher has made a cockroach stay in one place by chilling it in the freezer. He's gotten a fly to clean itself by dipping its head in honey. And for a horror movie, he's sent thousands of moths, mealworms, flies, and spiders shooting out of a dummy's stomach by loading them into a pipe and then shoving them out with a plunger.

For use with Step 5: Independent Application
last 2 paragraphs

Audiences may scream at Kutcher's insects in theaters, but Kutcher treats his bugs with love and care on the set. After completing a scene, he sucks his bugs up in specially built vacuums that don't hurt them and ensure that they don't get squashed later on.

When Kutcher's not working with insect movie stars, he's giving talks to kids and adults about appreciating bugs and protecting the environment we all live in. "I'm really concerned about the environment," Kutcher says. "And I'm very passionate about bugs."

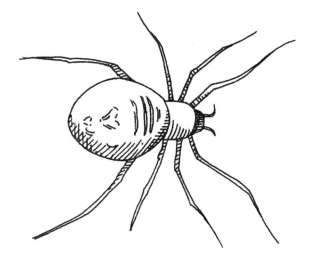

Drawing Inferences With Informational Text

GOAL • Help students understand how drawing inferences during and after reading can enhance comprehension of informational text

I Can Statement

I can draw inferences by using the Author & Me Inference Chart.

Reading Cycle & QAR

Reading Cycle: During and After Reading

QAR: *Author & Me:* Using author's clues to identify useful background knowledge and experiences for understanding informational text

Materials *(See CD for reproducibles.)*

▶ "The First Cowboys" by Sarah Jane Brian (informational passage), p. 57 (one copy for each student)

▶ Core QARs Poster (display copy)

▶ QAR and the Reading Cycle Poster (display copy)

(Refer to the posters as necessary during the lesson.)

▶ QAR Author & Me Inference Chart (display copy, one copy for each pair and for each student)

▶ QAR Self-Assessment Thinksheet (one copy for each student)

BEFORE READING   **DURING READING**   **AFTER READING**

Step **1** EXPLICIT EXPLANATION

Explain the purpose of today's lesson.

The focus of today's lesson is the comprehension strategy of drawing inferences, an important strategy that active readers use during and after reading all kinds of texts, including stories, poems, and informational text. An inference is something that readers figure out by using clues that the author provides in the text. An author cannot put every single detail readers need or want to know into a text, since that would make it very, very long and potentially very boring.

Display the following sentences and read them aloud: *James rushed to the breakfast table since he was running so late. His teacher had told him yesterday that he needed to be on time!* Ask students to think about what inferences they can make about James, the time of day, what James has been doing, or any other information that they think makes sense. Then give an example to start the process:

> *I can infer a lot of information that the author has not provided, but that as an active reader, I have figured out. For example, I think that it is morning and that James has woken up, maybe taken a shower, but certainly changed from his pajamas into clothes. What are some other things you think you know that the author did not explicitly tell us?*

Possible responses: James is going to school, since he is thinking of his teacher's comment; being on time is a problem for him; he was hungry, so his mom (dad, grandpa, aunt) did not let him leave the house without eating something. Underscore that there are many correct inferences active readers can draw when they read depending on their own experiences and knowledge, but inferences always have to make sense given the clues the author provides in the text.

> *As you can guess, the QAR for drawing inferences is Author & Me. Active readers ask themselves several questions while reading. In this lesson, we're going to be reading an informational text. Informational texts usually have been written to teach us something new or to persuade us of a certain point of view, so inferences usually have something to do with what new ideas we can learn from what the author tells us and from how we put authors' clues together.*
>
> *Active readers are constantly drawing inferences to help them understand the meaning of the text. To draw useful inferences when reading an informational text, I start by asking myself the following question: "How do the author's clues fit with my background knowledge and experiences?"*
>
> *If there's a good fit and my background knowledge and experiences seem useful, I can ask myself another question: "What inference can I make, using my background knowledge and experiences?"*
>
> *But sometimes there isn't a good fit between the author's clues and my background knowledge. Perhaps I don't have any useful background knowledge or my background knowledge is incomplete or inaccurate. In these cases, I need to ask myself a different question that helps me think about how I should put together the author's clues: "What inference can I make about a new idea to add to my knowledge?"*

Step **2** MODELING

Today I'm going to show you how to use a QAR Author & Me Inference Chart to draw inferences with an informational text. The QAR Author & Me Inference Chart has similar categories as the QAR Author & Me Prediction Chart, which you already know how to use. The first column heading, Author, reminds me to start with the author's clues. The second column heading, Me, reminds me to use my background knowledge and experiences to think about what I know that can help me understand the text. The third column, Inference, is where I write what I have figured out about the text.

Note:
If students have participated in Lesson 5 and are familiar with the QAR Author & Me Prediction Chart, make the connection to today's lesson, as indicated in the second sentence. If not, skip this sentence.

Once students have grasped the connections to QAR language, introduce the text.

When I make an inference, I start with the author's clues and think of how I can add useful information from my own background knowledge. The title of the text we are reading today is "The First Cowboys." This is a good clue, so I'm entering it in the Author column. Right away, I activate my background knowledge about cowboys and what they look like and do. I'll keep this background in mind as I read the text.

Continue by reading the first paragraph and modeling how to use the QAR Author & Me Inference Chart to make good inferences about the passage. Enter key words from the text in the Author column and information from your own experiences/knowledge in the Me column. Samples are in the chart below.

QAR Author & Me Inference Chart

AUTHOR	ME	INFERENCE
First cowboys Rides across the plains Hat with a wide brim Lasso swinging	Riding horses Rodeos Plains are big fields that don't have many trees. Cowboys swing ropes to catch cattle.	Wide brim on the hat is needed to protect cowboy from sun. Lasso is the name of the cowboy's rope.
Nothing more American Mexican		A lot of people think the first cowboys were American but they are wrong.

The author is giving me a lot of information about cowboys, like where they work (in the plains), what they wear (hat with a wide brim), and that they have something called a lasso that they swing. I have some information In My Head that I think might be helpful. I know the plains are huge open fields with hardly any trees, so one of my inferences is that the wide brim on the cowboy's hat can protect them from the sun. I'm not sure what a lasso is, but I know that I've seen cowboys in movies swinging ropes to catch cattle, so I bet that the name of the cowboy's rope is lasso. And, the author is telling me that there's nothing more American than a cowboy, but that the first cowboys were Mexican. I bet a lot of people think the first cowboys were American, but they are wrong!

Guide students to realize that active readers use the author's clues and then check their own background knowledge to draw inferences about what is happening in the text and what the author wants readers to understand.

Step **3** GUIDED PRACTICE

Display the text.

Now I want you to practice using the QAR Author & Me Inference Chart to draw inferences, following the same steps I've just modeled for you. I'm going to read the next section of text to you. While I read, your job is to help me think about the information that can be added to the three columns: clues from the author, our own background knowledge, and possible inferences.

Note:
Emphasize the process of logical thinking rather than of getting the right answer. Praise students who use sound logic even if they come up with unexpected ideas.

Read the next two paragraphs and then show the picture and read the caption. After you have finished reading, have students turn to a partner and discuss ideas that could go in each column of the chart. Ask partners to share their ideas and add them to the QAR Author & Me Inference Chart. The sample below can help you get started.

AUTHOR	ME	INFERENCE
Spanish people settled, bringing cows and horses	Cows—milk, meat Horses—transportation	Cows, horses, valuable to ranchers
Large, wild herds	Wild herds means cows, horses not being used by people.	Ranchers want to catch wild cows, horses. Use some, sell some

Step 4 COACHING

Hand out a copy of the passage to each student. Ask students to draw their own QAR Author & Me Inference Chart on a sheet of notebook paper and read the next section with a partner. They can take turns reading the text to each other and then work together to write two or more new inferences.

> *Remember to start by looking at how well the author's clues match the background knowledge you already have. If the two seem consistent, go ahead and draw an inference based on your background knowledge. If the two seem inconsistent, see if you can put clues from the author together to form a new idea that you might want to add to your knowledge.*

Allow partners time to read the text, discuss their thinking, and complete their individual QAR Author & Me Inference Charts. Provide coaching to students who experience difficulty by helping them think of the author's clues and the match or mismatch with their own background knowledge. Have partners share the inferences they made. Add their ideas to the class QAR Author & Me Inference Chart, remembering to praise students who show logical thinking. A sample for this section of the text appears below.

AUTHOR	ME	INFERENCE
Danger big part of job	Danger—have to be brave	Vaqueros had to be brave to do their job.

Step 5 INDEPENDENT APPLICATION

> *On your own, please read the remaining text, view the final photo, and read its caption. As you read, remember to start with the author's clues. Then see if you have any useful background knowledge that can help you draw an inference to further your understanding of the text. Add at least one new row of ideas under each of the headings in the chart: Author, Me, and Inference.*

Encourage students who finish early to add more entries to their chart. Invite a few students to add their entries to the class chart. Call the whole group back together and have several students share the entries from their QAR Author & Me Inference Chart. A sample chart entry for the final portion of the text appears below.

AUTHOR	ME	INFERENCE
Vaquero history—Mexican rodeos	American rodeos, barrel racing, bareback riding, other events?	Mexican rodeos—vaqueros competing in different kinds of events

Step **6** SELF-ASSESSMENT & GOAL SETTING

Display the I Can Statement and remind students of the purpose of the lesson.

> *The purpose of this lesson was to help you learn to draw inferences during and after reading to improve your comprehension of the text. We learned to draw inferences using the QAR Author & Me Inference Chart. Who can describe what you did when working with this chart?*

Call on two or three students to explain how they used the QAR Author & Me Inference Chart to draw inferences. Remind students that the author's clues sometimes help us realize that our background knowledge is inaccurate or incomplete. This is the case with informational texts such as "The First Cowboys," where the author would like readers to learn new ideas.

> *Now I would like you to think about how you can use the strategy of drawing inferences in other areas and how you can add inferences to your own personal toolkit for reading.*

Then have students complete their QAR Self-Assessment Thinksheet and turn it in with their QAR Author & Me Inference Chart.

The First Cowboys

By Sarah Jane Brian

For use with Step 2: Modeling

title and the first paragraph

A cowboy rides across the plains on a horse. He wears a hat with a wide brim and swings a lasso over his head as he herds cattle. To most people, nothing could seem more American. But the first cowboys weren't American. They were Mexican.

Horses and cows first came to North America on some of Christopher Columbus's ships. As Spanish people took over the land, cows and horses followed. Some animals escaped. They formed large wild herds. The herds traveled across the plains of Mexico and the area that later became the American Southwest.

For use with Step 3: Coaching

next 2 paragraphs and illustration with caption

Spanish ranchers hired workers to round up the wild cattle and horses. These workers were called *vaqueros* (bah-KEHR-ohs). The word "vaquero" comes from the Spanish word for cow, *vaca* (BAH-cah). Many vaqueros had a mixed Spanish and Native American heritage.

A vaquero from about 1900

A Life of Danger

For use with Step 4: Guided Practice

"A Life of Danger" heading and next 2 paragraphs

From the 1500s to the 1700s, vaqueros created special clothes and tools to help them do their jobs. They developed amazing skills in riding horses and roping cattle. Vaqueros learned to tame wild horses and kill grizzly bears that attacked their cattle. Danger was a big part of the job.

During the 1830s and 1840s, the U.S. won control of California, Texas, and the rest of the Southwest. Americans who came west knew little about cattle. Vaqueros taught them everything they had learned.

By the 1860s, most Americans who worked with cattle were called cowboys. They became known around the world for their skills, toughness, and bravery. Cowboys grew more famous, but it was the vaqueros who invented the cowboy way of life.

For use with Step 5: Independent Application

last 2 paragraphs and illustration and caption

Today there are still a few skilled men who work with horses and cattle and call themselves vaqueros. Vaquero history also lives on in Mexican rodeos.

A vaquero today

Drawing Inferences With Narrative Text

GOAL

● Help students understand how drawing inferences during and after reading can enhance comprehension of narrative texts

I Can Statement

I can draw inferences by the using an Author & Me Inference Chart.

Reading Cycle & QAR

Reading Cycle: During and After Reading

QAR: *Author & Me:* Using author's clues to identify useful background knowledge and experiences for comprehending narrative text

Materials *(See CD for reproducibles.)*

▶ "All in a Day's Work" by Megan Stine and H. William Stine (narrative passage), p. 65 (one copy for each student)

▶ Core QARs Poster (display copy)

▶ QAR and the Reading Cycle Poster (display copy)

(Refer to the posters as necessary during lesson.)

▶ QAR Author & Me Inference Chart (display copy, one copy for each pair and for each student)

▶ QAR Self-Assessment Thinksheet (one copy for each student)

| BEFORE READING | **DURING READING** | **AFTER READING** |

Step 1 EXPLICIT EXPLANATION

Begin by explaining the purpose of this lesson as suggested below. (If you have taught Lesson 7, about drawing inferences with informational text, you simply may want to remind students what it means to draw an inference, and note that in this lesson they will learn to draw inferences during and after reading a story.)

The focus of today's lesson is the comprehension strategy of drawing inferences, an important comprehension strategy that active readers use during and after reading. You have already learned about using this strategy with informational text, and now you will learn how to draw inferences when reading a narrative or story.

An inference is information that readers figure out by using clues that the author provides in the text. An author cannot put every single detail readers need or want to know in a text, since that would make it very, very long and potentially very boring. Let's look at these sentences together.

If students are new to drawing inferences or need further reinforcement of this strategy, introduce the activity below. (The framework of this activity appeared in Lesson 7.)

Tell students you will be looking at a narrative text to explore what it means to draw inferences. Display the following sentences and read them aloud:

Sam ran up to Alex, who had the biggest smile on her face, even though her hair was dripping wet and she was having trouble catching her breath. "This was a huge win for us—you were as smooth as a fish!" Sam told her.

Ask students to draw inferences about these sentences: what the sentences reveal about Sam and Alex, where this event is taking place, what Alex has been doing, or any other information they think makes sense. Give an example to start the process.

I can think of a lot of information the author has not provided, but that I can infer as an active reader. For example, I can draw the inference that Alex has just gotten out of the water—a pool, lake, or ocean—because she is dripping wet. What inferences were you able to draw about information that the author did not explicitly tell us?

Have students share their inferences and indicate the clues in the text that led to these inferences. [*Possible responses: Inference: She swam really hard. Clues: Her hair was dripping wet, and she was out of breath. Inference: She and Sam are on the same team, maybe a swim team. Clue: It was a huge win for them. Inference: Sam admires how she looked when she was swimming. Clue: He said she was "as smooth as a fish." Inference: Her victory may have made the difference in whether or not the team wins the meet. Clues: She was smiling, and Sam congratulated her.*]

Elicit the idea that active readers take the author's clues and use their own background knowledge and experiences to fill in information that the author did not provide. Underscore that there are many possible inferences active readers can draw when they read, depending on their own experiences and knowledge, but that inferences always have to make sense given the clues in the text.

The QAR for drawing inferences is Author & Me. Active readers ask themselves several questions while reading. In this lesson, we're going to be reading a story. Stories usually provide a way of thinking about our own lives, and they can also be like a window through which we can see what others' lives are like.

Active readers are constantly drawing inferences to help them understand the meaning of the text. To draw useful inferences when reading a narrative, I start by asking myself the following question: "What experiences have I had that might help me understand the story's characters, setting, events, or plot?"

Just as with informational texts, if there's a good fit and my background knowledge and experiences seem useful, I can ask myself another question: "What inference can I make, using my background knowledge and experiences?"

But sometimes while reading, I think, "Nothing like this has ever happened to me!" The story may be like a window into the lives of people, places, or events that I have never experienced. There isn't a good fit between the author's clues and the experiences I have had. In these cases, I need to ask myself a different question about the author's clues that helps me think about how I should put them together: "What inference can I make about a new idea to add to my knowledge?"

Step 2 MODELING

Today I'm going to show you how to use a QAR Author & Me Inference Chart to draw inferences. It has similar categories as the QAR Author & Me Prediction Chart, which you already know how to use. The first column heading, Author, reminds me to start with the author's clues. The second column heading, Me, reminds me to use my background knowledge and experiences to think about what I know that can help me understand the text. The third column, Inference, is where I write what I have figured out about the text.

Once students have grasped the connections to QAR language, introduce the text.

The title of the story we are reading today is "All in a Day's Work." Right away, I start thinking about my own experiences that might be relevant, even though I think the title is awfully general. The word "work" leads me to think

Note:
If students have participated in Lesson 5 and are familiar with the QAR Author & Me Prediction Chart, make the connection to today's lesson, as indicated in the second sentence. If not, skip the second sentence. Similarly, if students have participated in Lesson 7, review the information and invite them to supply some of the inferences with you.

about all the different kinds of work people do. I know what a day of work is like for a teacher. (Based on your own situation, add information about the workday of another adult, as well as for a "day of work" at home; for example: My brother is a psychologist, so I know that his day's work is a lot different from mine. And I think of a day's work at home on the weekend when I'm cleaning out the garage or fixing a broken light.)

Read the first paragraph of the text and then model how to use the QAR Author & Me Inference Chart to make good inferences about the story. You can record the underlined words in the script below in the appropriate column as you are thinking aloud, or after as you reflect on what you were thinking, but model how to write notes in the chart rather than copying the complete text.

When I make an inference, I start with the author's clues and think of how I can add useful information from my own background knowledge. When the author writes that Luisa was willing to "<u>do anything</u>" and "<u>summer job</u> I've spent <u>three weeks looking for</u>," I could relate that to how hard it was for me to find good summer jobs. The words "<u>clown costume</u>" made me think that this could be fun or embarrassing because it's not like it's Halloween and costumes are expected, and "stand in the street and <u>wave cars into the gas station</u>" surprised me since I've never heard of a grownup asking a kid to stand in the street, especially if he's the boss or owner because he's sending an employee into a dangerous situation.

QAR Author & Me Inference Chart

AUTHOR	ME	INFERENCE
do anything summer job 3 weeks looking for job	hard to get summer jobs	Luisa is a young person who is going to take a clown job at a gas station.
clown costume wave cars into station	dangerous to stand in the streets	weird boss?

Guide students to realize that active readers use the author's clues and then check their own background knowledge to draw inferences about what is happening in the text and what the author wants them to understand.

My inferences are that this story is about Luisa and her job working for a gas station, and that her boss or the job as a clown standing in the street might be a little weird or dangerous. I'll have to read more to see if my inferences are on the right track.

Step 3 GUIDED PRACTICE

Display the text.

> *Now I want you to practice using the QAR Author & Me Inference Chart to draw inferences, following the same steps I've just modeled for you. I'm going to read the next section of the story aloud. While I read, your job is to help me think about the information that can be added to the three columns: clues from the author, our own background knowledge, and possible inferences.*

Note:
Emphasize the process of logical thinking rather than of getting the right answer. Praise students who use sound logic even if they come up with unexpected ideas.

After you have finished reading, have students turn to a partner and discuss ideas that could go in each column of the chart. Ask partners to share their ideas and add them to the QAR Author & Me Inference Chart. The sample below can help you get started.

AUTHOR	ME	INFERENCE
boss says it will be fun	standing in street in a clown costume does not sound like fun	The boss doesn't know much about how to be a boss to a kid.
"look like a fool" fists tightened slowly opened door	hard to look silly in front of my friends	Luisa is not happy about this job, but she's brave to do it anyway.
50 new customers or "you're fired"	50 is a lot of customers!	Her boss is not very nice to kids.

Step 4 COACHING

Hand out a copy of the story and a QAR Author & Me Inference Chart to each student. Ask students to read the next section with a partner. They can take turns reading the story to one another and then work together to write two or more new inferences.

> *Remember to start by looking at how well the author's clues match the background knowledge and experiences you already have. If the two seem consistent, go ahead and draw an inference based on your background knowledge. If the two seem inconsistent, see if you can put clues from the author together to form a new idea that you might want to add to your knowledge.*

Allow partners time to read the text, discuss their thinking, and complete their individual QAR Author & Me Inference Chart. Provide coaching to students who experience difficulty by helping them think of the author's clues and the match or mismatch with their own background knowledge and experiences. Have partners share the inferences they made. Add their ideas to the class QAR Author & Me Inference Chart, remembering to praise students who show logical thinking. A sample for this section of the story appears below.

AUTHOR	ME	INFERENCE
Kids tease Luisa, and she teases back.	hard to be teased!	Luisa is brave and clever.
Luisa yells and does funny things. Customers come to see her and go to the station.	doing a good job—feel important and successful	Boss is happy about the new business. Luisa likes her job now, feels important and successful.

Step 5 INDEPENDENT APPLICATION

On your own, please read the remaining text. As you read, remember to start with the author's clues. Then see if you have any useful background knowledge that can help you draw an inference to further your understanding of the text. Add at least one new row with new ideas under the headings in the chart: Author, Me, and Inference.

Encourage students who finish early to add more entries to their charts. Invite a few students to add their entries to the class chart. Then call the whole group back together and have several students share the entries from their charts. A sample chart entry for the final portion of the text appears below.

AUTHOR	ME	INFERENCE
business booms, Luisa fired anyway Luisa moves to Sam's—his business booms, Grogan's drops without her	have to keep trying sometimes when the first thing doesn't work out	Grogan should have given Luisa a raise. She wouldn't have left to go to Sam's, and his business would still be booming.

Step **6** SELF-ASSESSMENT & GOAL SETTING

Display the I Can Statement and remind students of the purpose of the lesson.

> *The purpose of this lesson was to help you learn to draw inferences during and after reading to improve your comprehension of the text. We learned to draw inferences using the QAR Author & Me Inference Chart. Who can describe what you did when working with this chart?*

Call on a couple of students to explain how they used the QAR Author & Me Inference Chart to draw inferences. Remind them that stories help us reflect on our own lives and learn about the lives of others. Ask students to think about how the story, "All in a Day's Work," helped them gain a new perspective, think differently about their lives, or reinforce some of their own experiences and ways of thinking.

> *Now I would like you to think about how you can use the strategy of drawing inferences in other areas and how you can add drawing inferences to your own personal toolkit for reading.*

Then have students complete their QAR Self-Assessment Thinksheet and turn it in with their QAR Author & Me Inference Chart.

All in a Day's Work

By Megan Stine and H. William Stine

Use with Step 2: Modeling
title and first 6 paragraphs

"You want a job, kid?" asked Mr. Grogan.

"I sure do," said Luisa. "I'll do anything. I'll wash floors, change tires, pump gas—"

Mr. Grogan held up his hand. "No thanks. I've got enough kids at the gas pumps. I need more customers. So I've got an idea. I want you to dress up in a clown costume."

"A what?" asked Luisa.

"A clown costume. You'll stand in the street and wave cars into the gas station."

"This is the summer job I've spent three weeks looking for?" Luisa mumbled.

Use with Step 3: Guided Practice
next 5 paragraphs

Mr. Grogan pretended not to hear. "You can start tomorrow. It will be a lot of fun."

The next day, Luisa stood in front of the mirror. She had put on a red-and-white striped suit. Her face was all white with a big red nose. Her mouth was a fat red lipstick smear, and her eyebrows were big and blue.

"I look like a fool," Luisa said to herself. She put on an enormous green wig. She frowned into the mirror. Then, she slowly opened the door.

Mr. Grogan and his two helpers burst out laughing. Luisa's fists tightened.

"Kid," said Mr. Grogan, "remember our deal. If you don't get 50 new customers a week, you're fired. Now, get out there!"

Use with Step 4: Coaching
next 11 paragraphs

Luisa dragged her feet to the middle of the street. A car full of kids from the high school drove by. They stopped the car and stared at Luisa.

"Drive on into Grogan's," she said softly.

"You're early for Halloween," the driver said. "What are you supposed to look like?"

Luisa stared at him. "You, clown," she said.

The driver's face froze. The other kids in the car started laughing. "You know, Jack," one of the guys said to the driver, "you do look a little like her, especially late on Saturday nights." Then even the driver had to laugh.

"You may be laughing now, but wait until you see our prices," Luisa said.

The driver laughed again and spun the car into the gas station.

If it worked once, it could work again.

So Luisa started yelling different things as cars passed by.

"Drive that car into Grogan's before you have to push it in!"

"You've got enough dirt on that car to plant a garden. Drive into Grogan's for a car wash!"

Pretty soon, parents were driving by with their kids to see the clown. Luisa gave them balloons. She cleaned people's sunglasses instead of their windows. She made jokes.

By the end of the first week, Mr. Grogan's business was booming. At the end of the second week, Luisa asked Mr. Grogan for a raise.

"Are you kidding?" Mr. Grogan shouted.

"But I got you hundreds of new customers," Luisa said.

Use with Step 5: Independent Application
remainder of story

"Yeah, I know. Now that I have so many, who needs you? You're fired. Here's your pay. You can keep the clown costume."

At first, Mr. Grogan didn't notice. One by one, though, all of his customers disappeared. Then one day, he was driving down State Street, and traffic was really slow. "What's holding things up?" he grumbled. He blasted his horn, but no one moved. He got out of his car and stomped all the way to the corner.

There, in front of Sam's Service Station was Luisa. She was wearing her clown costume. She was telling everyone to "drive right on into Sam's!"

Business was booming.

Identifying Important Information in Informational Text

GOAL ● Help students understand how determining importance based on purposes for reading can enhance comprehension of informational text

I Can Statement

I can determine the important information in the text based on my purposes for reading.

Reading Cycle & QAR

Reading Cycle: Before, During, and After Reading

QAR: *Think & Search:* Using QAR Think & Search Important Information Chart to help guide students as they Think & Search text for information that is or might be important, given their guiding questions.

Materials *(See CD for reproducibles.)*

▶ "Waste Not, Want Not" by Susan Cosier (informational passage), p. 71 (one copy for each student)

▶ Core QARs Poster (display copy)

▶ QAR and the Reading Cycle Poster (display copy)

(Refer to the posters as necessary during the lesson.)

▶ QAR Think & Search Important Information Chart (display copy, one copy for each pair and for each student)

Note: Save the completed charts to use in Lesson 10 on summarizing informational text.

▶ QAR Self-Assessment Thinksheet (one copy for each student)

Step **1** EXPLICIT EXPLANATION

Let students know that the purpose of this lesson is learning to use the QAR Think & Search Important Information Chart to help organize and remember important text information. Remind them that before reading, active readers always have questions in mind to help them decide what is important in the text. Sometimes, these questions are provided for the reader—in the text or by the teacher. Other times, readers generate their own guiding questions to set their purpose for reading. Display the blank QAR Think & Search Important Information Chart.

Today I will be teaching you a useful tool that active readers use before reading, during reading, and after reading with informational text. This tool is called the QAR Think & Search Important Information Chart. "Think & Search" is in the name of the chart because this is the QAR that we use most often during reading of informational text. You might notice other types of QARs, too, but most often the QAR you use during reading will be Think & Search.

When we read informational text, our purpose is usually to learn something new. Before reading, we think about our purpose for reading, what it is we hope to learn. During reading, we keep our purpose in mind because it helps us figure out what is important to remember. After reading, we use the answers we've found to our questions to remember key ideas. We use these ideas for sharing what we've learned when we write summaries or describe the main ideas. The QAR Think & Search Important Information Chart can help you during all three parts of the reading cycle.

Step **2** MODELING

Sometimes, before-reading questions come from the text or someone gives them to me—such as when I am reading for a project or assignment. But many times I create my own guiding questions. I look at the title and other surface features of the text to get some ideas of the content, and then I make up questions that will help me keep in mind what I am hoping to learn.

The title of the passage we're going to read today is "Waste Not, Want Not." I see that the passage has two headings, "E-Waste Woes" and "Second Life." Between these three features (the title and the two headings), I should be able to create some questions that can be like a map to help me find important ideas in the text.

Enter each question in the chart as you think aloud (see sample chart on p. 79):

> *My first question is "What is e-waste?" I have some guesses, because I know that waste is like garbage, but I am not positive what "e-waste means." Second, I am guessing from the title and the word "woes" that the author does not think any waste is a good thing, so I wonder, "What kind of problem does e-waste in particular cause?" And from the words "second life," I'm curious if anyone is trying to solve the e-waste problem by reusing the waste somehow? My last question is "What solutions have been tried to solve the e-waste problem?"*

After entering the questions in the chart, read aloud the first sentence of the text and model how to write ideas in the other columns.

> *Listen carefully as I read the first sentence in the text and ask yourself if this information is important to any of my three questions. "Old computers are getting a second life after undergoing a makeover in Alex Lin's makeshift repair room in his family's basement." Let's see if we are thinking similar thoughts. I think that "old computers" gives me some important information about what e-waste is [enter "old computers" in column 2, important information], and I think the information about "undergoing makeover" and "repair room" may be important information about solutions to the problem. It may be that Alex Lin is important, so I'm also going to write his name down, just in case I need to remember it later. [Column 3 should now contain "undergoing makeover," "repair room," "Alex Lin."]*

Step 3 GUIDED PRACTICE

Distribute a copy of the passage to each student. Continue reading the next three paragraphs aloud, asking students to Think & Search as they code text information. Have them use an exclamation point (!) next to information they think IS important, and a question mark (?) next to information they think MIGHT BE important.
Note: For a more extensive lesson on coding for importance, see Lesson 9 in *QAR Comprehension Lessons, Grades 2–3*.

Then ask students to share information that they believe is definitely important, the question it relates to, and why they think this information is likely to be important. Enter this information in the chart. Continue asking students to share information that they think might be important, the related question, and their reasons for thinking this information might be important.

Ask for a volunteer to summarize what the class has learned so far (e.g., Q1: e-waste is electronic waste; Q2: landfills with e-waste are an environmental hazard; Q3: Alex and friends created WIN to repair and distribute computers to those who need them). Then continue reading, adding to the important information already in the chart. Remind students that as they read, they may decide to move information from the last column to the Very Important Information column or cross it out as unimportant.

Step **4** COACHING

Tell students that they will work with a partner. Together they will read, then Think & Search for information that is or that might be important to the three guiding questions on the class QAR Think & Search Important Information Chart.

> *With your partner, create a QAR Think & Search Important Information Chart that you can use to record your notes. Together, read the next section of the text to identify information that you can add to the chart according to the question it addresses. You might want to take turns, with one reading aloud and the other coding for important or possibly important information using the exclamation point and question mark codes.*

Circulate around the room to help students who need assistance with coding or making decisions about what is or might be important. Then bring students together to share. As they share ideas, ask them to explain their thinking. Have students indicate if they agree (and why) or disagree (and why) with the various suggestions. Ask them to revisit the last column to see if there is anything they want to move to the Very Important Information column or cross out. Enter important information in the appropriate column of the class chart as students share. Possible entries for information that IS important include:

▶ **Question 1:** e-waste contains hazardous elements

▶ **Question 2:** 2.25 million tons mostly in landfills, 80% shipped overseas; chemical leaks when improperly dumped in landfills, contaminates water; other countries suffer from the mess

▶ **Question 3:** reuse it; give it to someone who needs it

Step **5** INDEPENDENT APPLICATION

For independent practice, have students create a new Think & Search chart, read the remainder of the text, and identify and code information that IS or MIGHT BE important.

When students have completed the task, lead a discussion about the important information they read in the last section. Ask each student to put a star next to an idea he or she wants to share. Call on students to share one idea and the guiding question it fits, continuing until no one has an important idea that is not represented on the chart. Have students review the last column to see if an idea could be moved to the Very Important Information column or crossed out. Illustrative important ideas include the following:

▶ **Question 1:** contains some precious metals

▶ **Question 2:** we need to mine more metals if we don't recycle

▶ **Question 3:** refurbishing is a green option, refurbished computers have been sent all over the world to people who need them

Step **6** SELF-ASSESSMENT & GOAL SETTING

Display the I Can Statement and ask students to keep it in mind as they think about what they have learned. When they have completed their self-assessment, discuss what they have learned.

> *Let's talk about what you learned about identifying important information before and during reading. How did this help your understanding of the text? In what ways was the QAR Think & Search Important Information Chart helpful? Describe other settings where you can imagine using it to help you find and remember important ideas.*

Following this discussion, remind students that active readers Think & Search strategically to figure out and record the information they think is or might be important. Note that using a chart like this one helps active readers remember and use the information they've identified after reading when they write summaries or main idea statements (see Lessons 10 and 12). Remind students to add what they learned in this lesson to their personal toolkit for reading. Finally, collect their QAR Self-Assessment Thinksheet and completed chart.

Waste Not, Want Not

By Susan Cosier

Use with Step 2: Modeling
title and first sentence

Old computers are getting a second life after undergoing a makeover in Alex Lin's makeshift repair room in his family's basement.

Use with Step 3: Guided Practice
next 3 paragraphs

The restored computers are now in the hands of Sri Lankan students whose school was demolished in a tsunami in 2004. Thanks to 15-year-old Alex and other teens in the town of Westerly, Rhode Island, schools across the world are getting wired with good-as-new electronics.

Five years ago, Alex read a story about the increasing number of electronics that Americans throw away, known as electronic waste, or e-waste. He sensed an opportunity to keep electronics out of already over flowing landfills and help people in need at the same time.

Alex and his buddies founded a group called the Westerly Innovations Network (WIN). They repair and update computers that people no longer want. Then, the team donates the spiffed-up machines to people and schools.

Use with Step 4: Coaching
"E-Waste Woes" section

E-Waste Woes

Last year, residents of the United States disposed of 2.25 million tons of e-waste, according to the Environmental Protection Agency (EPA). Most of it went into landfills, but not necessarily local ones. Advocacy groups, like the Basel Action Network and the Silicon Valley Toxics Coalition, estimate that the U.S. ships up to 80 percent of its e-waste overseas, where it may be dumped or burned.

E-waste contains elements that are hazardous to the environment, like lead, mercury, and chromium. Some of them, such as cadmium, are carcinogens, or substances that can cause cancer in humans. These chemicals often leak out of electronics when they are improperly recycled, put in a landfill, or dumped. The toxins can trickle down into surrounding soil and contaminate drinking-water supplies.

Since the e-waste generated here in the U.S. can be shipped overseas, other countries often feel the brunt of our e-waste mess. "It's just not smart in the long run to put this stuff in landfills, even here in the U.S., where most of our landfills are carefully managed," says Clare Lindsay, a project director in the office of solid waste at the EPA. Alex agrees. "The best way to deal with e-waste [is] to reuse it or give it to someone who needs it," he says.

Use with
Step 5:
Independent
Application

"Second Life"
section

Second Life

Instead of tossing old electronics in the trash, people can recycle them. Most electronics have precious metals that can be removed and reused so fresh metals don't have to be mined from the earth—a process that can be harmful to the environment. But refurbishing (fixing and updating) electronics, as WIN does, is an even greener option. That way, new electronics don't have to be made from scratch, and old ones don't have to be recycled or thrown away, says Scott Matthews, a professor at Carnegie Mellon University in Pittsburgh who has been studying e-waste for 20 years.

During a recycling drive, WIN collected 10 metric tons (21,000 pounds) of electronics in just one day! Over the past five years, Alex and his team have fixed more than 300 machines and donated them to those in need.

Besides sending computers to students in Sri Lanka, they have also shipped them to nations like Mexico and Cameroon, where other WIN branches were formed. "When we started, we had no idea that we could get anything—even a single computer—overseas to help people," says Alex. "But it worked out."

Summarizing Informational Text

GOAL • Help students understand how to create
a summary for informational text

I Can Statement

I can write a summary of important ideas in informational text.

Reading Cycle and QARs

Reading Cycle: After Reading

QARs: *Think & Search:* Organizing the important information in the text

Author & Me: Using your own knowledge of how ideas can go together to create a clear and logical representation of the important ideas in the text

Materials *(See CD for reproducibles.)*

▶ "Waste Not, Want Not" by Susan Cosier (informational passage), p. 71 (one for each student)

▶ Core QARs Poster (display copy)

▶ QAR and the Reading Cycle Poster (display copy)

(Refer to the posters as necessary during lesson.)

▶ QAR Think & Search Important Information Chart (completed class chart from Lesson 9; also see sample chart on p. 79) (large display copy, one copy for each pair and each student)

▶ QAR Think & Search Summary Web (large display copy, one copy for each pair and for each student)

▶ QAR Think & Search Summary Draft (large display, one copy for each student)

▶ QAR Self-Assessment Thinksheet (one copy for each student)

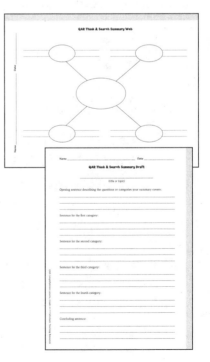

Step **1** EXPLICIT EXPLANATION

Explain the purpose of the lesson.

> *Today I'm going to teach you about a comprehension strategy called summarizing. Active readers most often summarize after reading to remember what they've read and share what they've read with others. When I finish reading a text, I often want to be sure that I remember the important information. When readers summarize, they include the important or big ideas the author wants them to understand, without worrying about all the details.*

> *When I summarize, I first identify the important information, just as you learned to do in earlier lessons. Then I organize the important information, which is easy to do if I use a web. Finally, I create a new brief text containing the important information—my summary. My summary is going to be much shorter than the original text, but it will capture the most important information.*

> *In Lesson 9, we practiced the first step when we figured out the important information in the passage, "Waste Not, Want Not." We will create our first summary using the QAR Think & Search Important Information Chart we completed for that article.*

> *Summarizing is a Think & Search QAR. After I search for what is important, I think about how to put the information together to create my brief new text—the summary of the passage.*

Step **2** MODELING

Display the following:

▶ Completed QAR Think & Search Important Information Chart for "Waste Not, Want Not" from Lesson 9

▶ QAR Think & Search Summary Web

▶ QAR Think & Search Summary Draft

Explain to students that you will show them how to use the QAR Think & Search Summary Web to organize the questions and important information in the QAR Think & Search Important Information Chart so they can easily create their new brief text—the summary.

Notice that our summary draft has four main parts. First there is a title or topic for the summary. Then there's an opening sentence that describes what will be in the summary. Next there are sentences about each main category. On this example, it shows three sentences, but there may be more or less depending on the amount of information in a passage and the number of categories the information fits into. The last part of a summary is the concluding sentence that brings the summary to an end.

Today we're going to create a summary for the passage we read in Lesson 9, "Waste Not, Want Not" by Susan Cosier. I'm going to use my QAR Think & Search Summary Draft as a guide. My first step is to make the topic of the summary really clear. Sometimes the title works, but "Waste Not, Want Not" could be about a lot of different things. Since the entire passage is about e-waste, I am going to enter that for the title of my summary. I'm going to write the author's name in parentheses (by Susan Closier) to remember that information.

Next, I am going to decide on how many categories of information I am going to include in my summary, using my ideas from my Important Information Chart. I know I had three questions that the passage helped me answer. These questions will be my information categories. For this summary, I can describe three types of things I learned about e-waste.

Point to the questions on the QAR Think & Search Important Information Chart and demonstrate how each of those questions can become a category.

The first question, "What is e-waste?" has information that describes what e-waste is. On the web, I'm going to name my first category "e-waste" description (enter on a line leading to one of the web hub circles).

Repeat for the remaining two categories, thinking aloud as you enter: "problems e-waste causes, solutions tried."

Now I have what I need to write my opening sentence. An easy way to create an opening sentence for an informational passage is to start with "This passage tells about…" and then tell the topic and the categories of information in the article. Using my topic and the three categories on my web, I will write, "This passage tells about e-waste, the problems it causes and some solutions to the problem." Since this is just a draft, I can revise my opening sentence later and make it a more interesting lead.

A good summary of informational text provides important information and leaves out less important details. Our QAR Think & Search Important Information Chart will help me know which ideas I will want to include in my summary. I will organize my summary around the three questions in the chart. As I think about the summary, I'll think about an order that makes sense. For this summary, it makes sense to follow the order of the article—first telling what it is, then the problems it causes, and finally the solutions that have been tried.

My next step is to decide on the important information from each category that I need to include to have a clear, concise summary. For each question, I'll read through the information that I thought was important and write down phrases that will help me remember the idea. These ideas will be what I use to write my summary in my own words.

Model reducing the information in column 2 of the QAR Think & Search Important Information Chart down to just the essential points. (See sample chart on p. 79.) For each category, enter the phrases that capture the key idea next to the relevant oval on the web, beginning with the information to describe the first category, what e-waste is.

All this information helped me understand what e-waste is, but I don't need all of it to describe e-waste. I think it's important to include that "e" stands for electronic and that the waste is hazardous (enter underlined phrases in the Web on the lines extending from "e-waste description"). I will also include "has precious metals," since I learned that not reusing these metals means we dig up the earth to mine more, and that is a big problem. I won't include the information about causing cancer, since it gives an example about "hazardous," but it doesn't add to an explanation of e-waste. Now I have what I need to write my summary sentence for the first category.

Show how to convert the information answering the first question into a sentence you can use in the summary, and copy it on the QAR Think & Search Summary Draft (e.g., "E-waste is electronic waste that includes precious metals but is hazardous to the environment.")

Step **3** GUIDED PRACTICE

Point out that you now have your topic, opening sentence, and a sentence for your first category of information for your summary. Explain to students that you would like them to help you create the next sentence. Refer to the summary web and elicit the name of the next category of information, problems e-waste causes. Draw students' attention to the chart. Read through the list of important information, and ask students to indicate the points they think are most important. Elicit central ideas and enter them on the lines for the oval labeled "problems" (e.g., millions of tons in landfills, chemical leaks in the landfills can contaminate water, not using the precious metals leads to unnecessary mining). Note the information that you decided not to include and why (e.g., the numbers 2.25 and 80%, since you are already including the idea of quantity by saying "millions," "other countries suffer" since your summary topic is e-waste overall, which includes all countries).

Step 4 COACHING

Distribute a copy of a QAR Think & Search Summary Web and a QAR Think & Search Summary Draft to each student. Ask students to enter information for the second category on their own summary web so that it matches the one you are modeling, and to write the title, opening sentence, and sentence for the first category on their QAR Think & Search Summary Draft. Explain that they will need this for the next step.

> *You and a partner are going to create your sentence for the problems caused by e-waste. Start by looking at your web and keeping that category in mind. Then look at the key ideas on your summary web on the lines that go with the kinds of problems that are caused by e-waste. With your partner, create a sentence that captures the kinds of problems.*

When they have finished, ask pairs to form a square (2 pairs, 4 students) and share their sentences. Ask them to compare what is similar and what was different about each of their examples, and what they can learn from seeing each other's sentences. Have a few students share their sentences, then ask them to add a sentence for this category to their summary drafts. Add a sample sentence that captures the key information for this category to the class chart (e.g., "E-waste causes three problems: (1) it takes up space in the landfills, (2) chemicals from e-waste can contaminate drinking water, and (3) extra mining takes place when we don't reuse precious metals").

Step 5 INDEPENDENT APPLICATION

If you have not already done so, distribute students' individual QAR Think & Search Important Information Charts from Lesson 9, or direct their attention to the completed class chart that is on display.

> *Now you will be working independently using the Important Information Chart from Lesson 9 to complete your summary web and your summary draft. Look at the category for the third question. Using the lines next to the third category in your web, enter the important information from the chart that you want to use in your summary. Use the category name and the phrases that capture the important information to create your next sentence for your summary draft.*

Briefly model the closing sentence and ask students to create a final sentence to end their summary.

An informational summary concluding sentence can be a brief statement of what you learned from the passage, such as, "E-waste is a problem we need to solve," or "E-waste is a challenge to the future." Think about one big idea you learned from the passage and create your final sentence to share that idea with your reader.

Again, monitor students and provide guidance as needed. When students are working with their webs, make sure that they are able to use the category to identify key points (e.g., reuse computers, repair computers). Provide assistance to students who are having difficulty with the wording of a sentence (e.g., "A good solution for e-waste is to repair and reuse computers.").

Then bring the group together. Call on two or three students to share the information they entered in their summary web, the sentence they composed for the third category, and their concluding sentence for their summary draft.

Step 6 SELF-ASSESSMENT & GOAL SETTING

Have students discuss what they learned about creating a summary. Be sure they understand that creating a summary requires three steps: (1) identifying the important information, which they accomplished with the QAR Think & Search Important Information Chart, (2) organizing the important information, which they accomplished with the summary web, and (3) writing a brief new text containing the important information, which they accomplished with the summary draft.

Display the I Can Statement and ask students to keep the statement in mind as they think about what they have learned.

Finally, tell students to complete the QAR Self-Assessment Thinksheet and turn it in with their completed web and draft.

Summarizing is a complex process that can prove challenging for many students. The more opportunities they have to practice summarizing, the better. Have students practice using their tools for summarizing in a range of disciplinary contexts. Social studies and science texts provide excellent opportunities for extended practice in summarizing important information.

Note:
This lesson shows students how to create a draft of a summary. You can build on this foundation by having them revise the draft to create a more polished summary. For example, guide students to write an interesting lead and to add a concluding sentence.

QAR Think & Search Important Information Chart

(Sample for Lesson 9)

QUESTION	VERY IMPORTANT INFORMATION	INFORMATION THAT MIGHT BE IMPORTANT, BUT I'M NOT SURE YET
What is e-waste?	Old computers Electronic waste Has hazardous elements, some of which can cause cancer Have precious metals that could be useful	Undergoing makeover Repair room Alex Lin Elements in e-waste: lead, mercury, chromium, cadmium Some of the elements can cause cancer (!)
What kind of problem does e-waste in particular cause?	Landfills with e-waste are an environmental hazard 2.25 million tons mostly in landfills, 80% shipped overseas Chemicals leak when improperly dumped in landfills and contaminate water Other countries suffer from the mess We have to mine more precious metals because we throw away the ones in the e-waste	Computers in landfills leak (!) Landfills in the U.S. are carefully managed. Refurbishing means fixing and updating
What solutions have been tried to solve the e-waste problem?	WIN is a group that repairs and distributes computers to those who need them Reuse computers Give them to someone who needs it Refurbishing computers is a green option (good for environment) Refurbished computers have been sent all over the world	Restored computers are in Sri Lanka, Mexico, and Cameroon WIN stands for Westerly Innovations Network Scott Matthews is a professor who has studied e-waste for 20 years

Note:

There may be slight variations between this chart and the one your class produced in Lesson 9, so use your judgment about whether to use it as is, or create a version that includes additional important information that your class discussed. All the think-alouds in this lesson use the information presented in this chart.

Identifying Important Information in Narrative Text

GOAL • Help students understand how determining importance based on purposes for reading can enhance comprehension of narratives

I Can Statement

I can determine the important information in the text based on my purposes for reading.

Reading Cycle & QAR

Reading Cycle: Before, During, and After Reading

QAR: *Think & Search:* Close reading for author clues

Materials *(See CD for reproducibles.)*

▶ "Owen Watts and the Horrible Historian" by Lauren Tarshis (narrative passage), p. 86 (one for each student)

▶ Core QARs Poster (display copy)

▶ QAR and the Reading Cycle Poster (display copy)

(Refer to the posters as necessary during lesson.)

▶ QAR Think & Search Important Information Chart (display chart, one for each pair and for each student)

▶ QAR Self-Assessment Thinksheet (one for each student)

BEFORE READING   DURING READING   AFTER READING

Step 1 EXPLICIT EXPLANATION

Tell students that today's lesson focuses on learning to read stories closely to look for clues about important information. Today's story is a character-driven mystery, so the important clues will relate to the key characters in the story. Students will learn to use the QAR Think & Search Important Information Chart to keep track of important information about the characters that they will use to solve the mystery.

If you have led students through Lesson 9, where they were taught to use the QAR

Think & Search Important Information Chart with informational text, establish the connection.

> *In our previous lesson, you learned how to use a QAR Think & Search Important Information Chart with informational text. Today I will be teaching you how to use this chart to identify important information when reading stories or narratives.*

> *Authors make their stories work well by using story elements such as character, setting, problem, and solution. The story we are reading today is a mystery. It is an example of a story where the characters are very important, and reading closely for details about them will help us solve the mystery. We'll use the QAR Think & Search Important Information Chart to take notes so we can remember details about the characters as we try to solve the mystery.*

Display the QAR Think & Search Important Information Chart.

> *The QAR Think & Search Important Information Chart is used for keeping track of the important information needed to understand what is happening in the story and why. You can use it before, during, and after reading stories. Before reading, we think about what we know about the type of story we are about to read and the kind of information it is likely to contain. Knowing that we'll be reading a mystery today already gives me some ideas about what to expect in the text. During reading, we think about what we are learning about the various story elements, such as the characters and setting. With the mystery we're reading today, we'll keep track of the important text information that might provide clues for solving it. After reading, we'll use information from our chart to solve it.*

Step 2 MODELING

Ask students what they know about the mystery genre that would help them determine important text information (e.g., a detective type of character, a mystery to be solved, things are not always what they seem).

Lead students to understand that the main questions we have when we read this genre are "What is the mystery?" and "How is the mystery solved?" Write these questions in the first column of the chart.

QAR Think & Search Important Information Chart

QUESTION	VERY IMPORTANT INFORMATION	INFORMATION THAT MIGHT BE IMPORTANT, BUT I'M NOT SURE YET
What is the mystery?		
How is the mystery solved?		

Display the title and first four paragraphs of the text, so students can see it and follow along as you do your coding.

> *Now I want to start thinking about story elements, starting with the characters. I start with the question, "Who are the important characters?" (Add this question to the first column of the chart.) I'm going to read and code the important information as I go along. I'll use an exclamation point next to information that I think is very important and a question mark next to information that I think might be important.*

Read the title and think aloud about it. Show students how you are coding the text with exclamation points and question marks.

> *I'll start by looking only at the title, which often gives me very important information. The title, "Owen Watts and the Horrible Historian," suggests that there are two characters in the story who could be important. I'll put an exclamation point next to each name. Now I'll write this information in our Important Information Chart. I'll write each name on a separate line so I'll have room to record what I'm learning about each character.*

> *As I read, I will watch for information about these two characters to learn who they are and see if they continue to be important. There may be other characters, so let me add the question, "Who are the other characters?" Another question I have is about where this story takes place: "What is the setting?"*

QUESTION	VERY IMPORTANT INFORMATION (!)	INFORMATION THAT MIGHT BE IMPORTANT, BUT I'M NOT SURE YET (?)
What is the mystery?		
How is the mystery solved?		
Who are the important characters?	Owen Watts	
	Horrible Historian	
Who are the other characters?		
What is the setting?		

As you read the story aloud, continue to code while pointing out what you are noticing about the characters.

> Owen Watts is " . . . nosy. A snoop. Into everyone's business." (Add exclamation points next to this information in the text.) *I think that he is going to be a main character. The author starts the story with him, so the author is giving me some clues that could be important—"Owen is nosy!" I think that is an important thing to know about him when there's a mystery at hand.*

Write the important information you coded with an exclamation point on the Important Information Chart. Also add information coded with a question mark. See the sample chart below.

QUESTION	VERY IMPORTANT INFORMATION (!)	INFORMATION THAT MIGHT BE IMPORTANT, BUT I'M NOT SURE YET (?)
What is the mystery?		
How does the mystery get solved?		
Who are the important characters?	Owen Watts, nosy, snoop, into everyone's business, can solve mysteries	Curious, not liked by everyone
	Horrible Historian	
Who are the other characters?	Maggie, Marco	
What is the setting?	School	

Review the information on the chart and wonder aloud about the Horrible Historian, the mystery, and how it is going to be solved.

Step 3 GUIDED PRACTICE

Distribute a copy of the passage to each student.

> *Now you'll have a chance to practice identifying important information from our mystery. I'm going to read the next section of the mystery to you. As I read, please follow along and code the text as you've just seen me do. Use an exclamation point next to information that you think is very important and a question mark next to information that you think might be important. The coding you do will help us know what to add to our Important Information Chart.*

Read the next section aloud, pausing after each phrase or sentence to give students a chance to code the text. Then ask students to share the following: (1) new characters to add to the chart (Mrs. Washington, Mrs. Jukes) and (2) important information (Mrs. Jukes: special visit, had a famous grandfather named Jeremiah who invented recycling; Mrs. Washington: met Mrs. Jukes recently, had not heard of her grandfather).

Step 4 COACHING

Hand out a blank copy of the QAR Think & Search Important Information Chart to each student. Allow time for students to copy the questions in the first column of the class chart onto their individual charts. Tell them they need not enter the information in the other columns at this time.

Pair students to work together. One partner is to play the part of the narrator, while the other is to read the dialogue spoken by the characters. After partners have finished reading, they should discuss the text and code it with exclamation points and question marks. Then partners should add information coded with exclamation points to the second column of their charts and information coded with question marks to the third column. Remind them to jot notes rather than complete sentences. As students work, circulate around the room, offering assistance as needed, and identify partners who are doing an especially good job with the task.

When students have finished this task, call on two or three pairs you identified to share what they think should be added to the class chart, based on their coding. This information could include the following: (1) Mrs. Jukes: raising money for the Museum of Recycling in honor of grandfather Jedediah, fed horses, climbed trees to pick strawberries, (2) Mrs. Washington: looked at her lunch bag, (3) Students: doodled, fidgeted, (4) Owen: paid close attention.

Step **5** INDEPENDENT APPLICATION

Tell students that it is time for them to practice identifying important information in the mystery on their own, using the remainder of the text. Remind them that they will now have the opportunity to answer the first two questions in the chart: "What is the mystery?" "How does the mystery get solved?"

Once again, circulate around the room, offering assistance and looking for students who are doing an especially good job with the task.

BEFORE READING   DURING READING   **AFTER READING**

Step **6** SELF-ASSESSMENT & GOAL SETTING

Ask students to look at their individual QAR Think & Search Important Information Charts for answers to the main questions readers have when reading a mystery. Students' responses should be along the following lines: "The mystery was that Mrs. Jukes wasn't a real historian."

Proceed to the question of how the mystery got solved. Call on students to identify the four clues Owen noticed that helped him know that Mrs. Jukes was a fraud (calls her grandfather Jeremiah, then Jedediah; strawberries don't grow on trees; she is raising money for the Museum of Recycling but throws her plastic water bottle in the trash; she claims to be from Oakville yet has an Oakville map in her purse).

Lead students in a brief discussion of what they learned about identifying important information in a mystery or story. Guide them to think of how they can use what they learned in other settings.

> *Let's talk about what you learned about identifying important information before, during, and after reading of this mystery story. Did coding and the QAR Think & Search Important Information Chart help you understand the text? Why (or why not)? Describe other settings where you can imagine using coding and the QAR Think & Search Important Information Chart to help you find and remember important ideas.*

Tell students that they will be returning to the chart for a future lesson on summarizing a story. Be sure to save this chart as it will be needed in Lesson 12. Collect and save students' individual charts for use in Lesson 12 as well.

Display the I Can Statement and ask students to keep it in mind as they think about what they have learned. Then give students time to complete their QAR Self-Assessment Thinksheet and collect those.

Owen Watts and the Horrible Historian

By Lauren Tarshis

Can You Solve This Mystery?

For use with Step 2: Modeling

title, opening question and direction, first 4 paragraphs

Read this story VERY carefully, or else you could miss important clues.

Owen Watts is nosy. A snoop. Into everyone's business. At home, he's always listening at walls and peering through keyholes. At school, he strains to hear whispered conversations and cranes his neck to read secret notes. Not everyone appreciates Owen's natural curiosity.

"Stand back, Owen!" says Maggie when he tries to listen in on the girls' lunch chatter.

"Back off, Owen!" says Marco when Owen eyes the grade on Marco's spelling test.

But the kids never get too mad at Owen. Because when there's a mystery to solve in class, they know they can count on Owen Watts to save the day.

For use with Step 3: Guided Practice

next 4 paragraphs

Like on a certain Monday in January, when a special visitor came to speak to their class.

"This is Mrs. Jukes," said their teacher, Mrs. Washington. "She and I met at an Oakville History Club event." (Mrs. Washington loved history almost as much as she loved food.)

"Yes!" said Mrs. Jukes. "My grandfather, Jeremiah Jukes, was a famous farmer here. He practically invented recycling."

"I was surprised I'd never heard of Mr. Jukes before our special visitor told me about him," Mrs. Washington said to the class.

For use with Step 4: Coaching

next 3 paragraphs

"That's why I decided to come talk to all of you today—to spread the word about him," replied Mrs. Jukes. "I'm also raising money for the Museum of Recycling, in honor of my dear grandfather, Jedediah Jukes. We were so close."

For the next 30 minutes, Mrs. Jukes talked about her grandfather. Most kids fidgeted and doodled. Mrs. Washington eyed her lunch bag. But Owen paid close attention.

"Oh, the memories of the farm," Mrs. Jukes said. "Feeding the horses, climbing trees to pick strawberries . . . just thinking of it makes me weepy."

For use with Step 5: Independent Application

remainder of story

She opened her purse. Owen peeked in, surprised by the mess of papers, a plastic water bottle, and a map of Oakville. Mrs. Jukes reached for a tissue and the water bottle. She tossed the bottle into the trash and dabbed her eyes. Then, she picked up a pile of envelopes stacked in front of her.

"Please bring these home to your parents," she sniffed, passing them out. "If every family donates $20 for the museum, we can . . ."

"Excuse me," Owen said. "We shouldn't give this woman a penny."

"Owen!" Mrs. Washington gasped.

"She's a fraud!" Owen said. "And I can prove it."

Can you find the four clues that prove Mrs. Jukes is a phony?

Summarizing Narrative Text

GOAL • Help students understand how to create a summary for a narrative text

I Can Statement

I can write a summary of important ideas in narrative text.

Reading Cycle & QARs

Reading Cycle: After reading

QARs: *Think & Search:* Organizing the important information in the text

Author & Me: Using your own knowledge of how ideas can go together to create a clear and logical representation of the important ideas in the text

Materials *(See CD for reproducibles.)*

▶ "Owen Watts and the Horrible Historian" by Lauren Tarshis (narrative passage), p. 86 (one for each student)

▶ Core QARs Poster (display copy)

▶ QAR and the Reading Cycle Poster (display copy)

(Refer to the posters as necessary during lesson.)

▶ QAR Think & Search Important Information Chart (completed class chart from Lesson 11; also see sample chart on p. 83) (large display copy, one copy for each pair and each student)

▶ QAR Think & Search Summary Web (large display copy, one copy for each pair and each student)

▶ QAR Think & Search Summary Draft (large display copy, one copy for each pair and for each student)

▶ QAR Self-Assessment Thinksheet (one copy for each student)

BEFORE READING   DURING READING   **AFTER READING**

Step 1 EXPLICIT EXPLANATION

When you explain the focus of this lesson, include the first sentence below only if you've taught Lesson 10, on summarizing of informational text.

> *You've already learned to summarize informational text, and today you will be learning to summarize a story or narrative. Summarizing is*

an important comprehension strategy used after reading. When readers summarize, they include the most important ideas the author wants them to understand, without worrying about all the details.

I will be teaching you how to summarize a story by returning to the mystery we read earlier, "Owen Watts and the Horrible Historian." When readers summarize, they must first identify the important information. We completed this step when we filled in our QAR Think & Search Important Information Chart for this story, so we will use this chart as the basis for our summary.

After identifying the important information, the other two steps in summarizing are to organize the important information and then to create a brief new text—the summary of the story.

Step **2** MODELING

Display the following:

▶ QAR Think & Search Summary Web

▶ QAR Think & Search Summary Draft

▶ completed QAR Think & Search Important Information Chart for "Owen Watts and the Horrible Historian" from Lesson 11

If students participated in Lesson 10, remind them that these are the same graphic organizers they used to summarize informational text. Explain that you will show them how to use the QAR Think & Search Summary Web to organize important information in the story. The web will help you organize the questions and important information in the chart to help organize ideas for the summary. Then you will show them how to use the QAR Think & Search Summary Draft to start writing their brief new text— the summary.

I'm going to start with the topic, or title, of the summary. In the center of the QAR Think & Search Summary Web, I'll enter the title and author, "Owen Watts and the Horrible Historian" by Lauren Tarshis, because that is what this summary will be about. Now I'll go to my QAR Think & Search Summary Draft. I think it would be a good idea to use the same title, so I'll copy it here. Below the title I'm going to add the opening sentence—a sentence that describes what this summary is about. An easy way to create an opening sentence for a story summary is to start with "This story is about . . ." I'll write: "This story is about a woman who is pretending to be a historian." This is a draft, and I can revise the sentence later to include an interesting lead.

A good story summary, like a good summary of informational text, provides important information and omits the less important details. It fits our expectations that stories have predictable elements, such as characters, setting, problem, and solution. We can organize our story summary around these elements.

Refer to the completed QAR Think & Search Important Information Chart you created in Lesson 11. Indicate to students that the chart includes the ideas they had decided were important in understanding the story and that the goal now is to decide which ones are useful in creating the story summary.

> *Now I'm going to use the QAR Think & Search Summary Web to organize the ideas from our Important Information Chart. I'll use the story elements in the chart as the categories for my web: setting, main characters, problem, and solution.*

Write each element in one of the ovals radiating from the center oval in the web. Be sure students understand that the categories in the summary web do not have to be in the same order as the questions on the Important Information Chart.

> *Notice that I didn't put the categories in the web in the same order as they appear on the Important Information Chart. I started my web with the setting and main characters, rather than with the problem and solution. I did this because I need to explain the setting and the characters in my summary before I can explain the mystery or problem and how it was solved.*

Refer to the Important Information Chart, and add information about the setting to the summary web. Then model how you write a sentence about the setting to add to the summary draft.

> *Now that I have information about the setting in the first oval in my summary web, I can take that information and turn it into a sentence for my summary draft. Let me see, I think I'll write: "The mystery takes place at Owen Watts's school."*

Step **3** GUIDED PRACTICE

Point out that you now have two sentences for your summary: the opening sentence and a sentence about the setting. Explain to students that you would like them to help you create the next sentence. Referring to the summary web, call students' attention to the oval with lines to add information about the main characters.

> *Let's think together about the next category of information in our summary web—the main characters. Take a look at what we wrote about the characters in our Important Information Chart and tell me what you think we should enter in our summary web.*

Have students suggest information about the main characters that should be put in the web, such as: Mrs. Washington, Owen's teacher; Mrs. Jukes, the woman claiming to be a historian; Owen Watts, the student who is good at solving mysteries. Write this information on the web in the section for main characters.

Call students' attention to the summary draft. Ask them to turn to a partner and discuss a sentence about the main characters that can be added to the summary draft. Have a few students share their sentences. Then write a sentence that the group agrees captures key information about the main characters, such as: "The two important characters in this story are Owen Watts, a student who is good at solving mysteries, and Mrs. Jukes, a woman who is pretending to be a historian."

Step 4 COACHING

Pass out a copy of a QAR Think & Search Summary Web and a QAR Think & Search Summary Draft to each student. Have students add information to their individual charts so that it matches the one you are modeling, explaining that they will need this when they work on their own later. For the next part of the task, students will work with their partners again.

> *You and your partner will now go on to the next category in the summary web, which is about the problem or mystery. Start by referring to ideas about the problem or mystery in the Important Information Chart. Write the key ideas in your summary web. Then work with your partner to think of a sentence about the problem. Add your sentence to the summary draft.*

Monitor the progress of the pairs and be sure to provide coaching as needed. Students may try to transfer too much information to their summary web. If this happens, have partners select just two or three ideas to transfer. If students have difficulty composing a summary sentence, suggest that they start with the words "The problem was . . ." A possible sentence is: "The problem was that Mrs. Jukes was acting like a historian so people would give her money." When pairs have completed their summary sentence, have them form a "square" (2 pairs, 4 students). Ask the squares to compare the information about the problem in their summary webs, as well as the sentences about the problem in their summary drafts.

Then bring the group back together. Ask two or three squares to share the similarities and differences they observed when comparing their summary webs and summary drafts.

Step 5 INDEPENDENT APPLICATION

Students will work independently to summarize the important information from the last category in the web—the solution.

> *Now you will be working independently with your summary web and summary draft. You will be looking at the last category, the solution or how the problem was solved. Review the ideas about the solution in the Important Information Chart, and then enter the important information about the*

solution in your summary web. Add a sentence to your summary draft that captures this important information.

Monitor students and provide assistance as needed. When students are working with their webs, make sure that they are being selective about the information entered. Provide assistance to students who may have difficulty with wording the sentence, suggesting that they begin with the words "The problem was solved when . . ."

Then call the group back together. Ask several students to share the information they entered in their summary web and the sentence they composed for their summary draft. A possible sentence about the solution might be: "The problem was solved when Owen used four clues to prove that Mrs. Jukes was a fraud." Guide students to the understanding that in a summary, it is not necessary to present details about the four clues. Also point out that in summarizing a narrative, a closing sentence may not be needed, since the final sentence of the summary explains the overall point of the story —solving the problem.

Step **6** SELF-ASSESSMENT & GOAL SETTING

Have students discuss what they learned about summarizing. Explain that summarizing a story or narrative requires the same three steps as summarizing an informational text: (1) identifying the important information, which can be accomplished by using an Important Information Chart, (2) organizing the important information, which can be accomplished by using a summary web, and (3) writing a brief new text containing the important information, which can be accomplished by using a summary draft.

Display the I Can Statement and ask students to keep the statement in mind as they think about what they have learned.

> *Think about how you could use summarizing in other areas and how you can add this strategy to your personal toolkit for reading. Please complete your QAR Self-Assessment Thinksheet and turn it in with your summary web and summary draft.*

Summarizing is a valuable yet challenging strategy for many students. Reinforce summarizing skills with narrative texts during language arts instruction, for authentic purposes, such as student book talks or book sales to encourage others to read a favorite book, for reading log entries in a multiple text unit, and in social studies when reading informational storybooks or informational texts using narrative structures (e.g., textbook sections using narrative to describe historical events in which problems are identified and solutions presented).

Note:
This lesson shows students how to create the draft of a story summary. You can build on this foundation by having them revise the draft to create a more polished summary. For example, guide students to rework their opening sentence to create a lead that will grab their readers' attention. Guide students to add a concluding sentence.

Questioning With Informational Text

GOAL ● Help students understand how to generate and respond to questions appropriate to each phase of the reading cycle

I Can Statement

I can ask and answer appropriate questions before, during, and after reading.

Reading Cycle & QARs

Reading Cycle: Before, During, and After Reading

QARs: *Right There:* Identifying important information
Think & Search: Connecting ideas across text
Author & Me: Making text-to-self connections
On My Own: Brainstorming prior to reading

Materials *(See CD for reproducibles)*

▶ "Polar Bear Nation" by Kristin Lewis (informational passage), p. 98 (one copy for each student)

▶ Core QARs Poster (display copy)

▶ QAR and the Reading Cycle Poster (display copy)

(Refer to the posters as necessary during lesson.)

▶ QAR Reading Cycle Chart (display copy, one copy for each pair and for each student)

▶ QAR Self-Assessment Thinksheet (one copy for each student)

Step 1 EXPLICIT EXPLANATION

Tell students that most of the time questioning in school means they are answering questions the teacher or the text has asked of them. However, we often learn as much, if not more, by creating our own questions as we read.

Today I'm going to teach you how to ask—not just answer—appropriate questions before, during, and after reading. The focus of today's lesson is on how to use these questions strategically throughout the reading cycle.

Step 2 MODELING

Display the QAR Reading Cycle Chart. Tell students that you will be using the QAR Reading Cycle Chart to help you keep track of three things: (1) the questions you have created for each phase of the reading cycle, (2) the QAR you think will be most helpful in answering the question, and (3) the information you think would contribute to a good answer for the question.

Refer to the QAR and the Reading Cycle Poster. Remind students that when we ask questions to support our comprehension, we use different QARs during each phase of the reading cycle. Elicit the three phases: before reading, during reading, and after reading (or, if necessary, prompt students using the poster). Have students explain why the QARs identified in the poster are appropriate to that particular phase of the reading cycle. Guide them to remember or understand the cycle: generating background knowledge and prediction (On My Own/Author & Me) before reading, using text information and making connections during reading (Right There, Think & Search, Author & Me), and reflecting on their connections to the text and the influence of the text on their thinking after reading (Author & Me). For example, you could say something like this:

> **Note:**
> We recommend completing Lesson 4 before this lesson. Then you can begin by reminding students to think about what they have learned about QARs and the reading cycle. Let students know that in this lesson you are focusing on question-asking with informational text.

Active readers create questions that help them think more deeply about what they are reading. We've learned that before reading a new text or text section, questions help us brainstorm what we know that could help us understand the text and focus our attention on what the text might be about. Questions can help us review important ideas once we have finished reading a whole text. Questions support our understanding throughout the reading cycle.

Before reading, I want to ask On My Own questions that will help me think about what I know that might help me understand the text. (In the Before-Reading Questions section of the chart, enter On My Own under QAR.) I'm going to use the QAR Reading Cycle Chart to organize my questions and keep track of my answers.

I'll start by looking at the title of the passage, "Polar Bear Nation"—something active readers do when they are selecting something to read. They look at the title of a book, an article, or a story to decide if it interests them. I might start with an On My Own QAR to get me brainstorming everything I know that could relate to this passage. The title makes me think this will be about polar bears, which I've seen at the zoo and on TV. I can picture the huge white bears. They look cuddly, but I have learned they are dangerous. I know they eat seals and other sea animals. On My Own QARs before reading help me brainstorm general information that I already know or think about personal experiences—like my trip to the zoo—that can help me understand the passage.

I know that Author & Me QARs before reading help me focus my attention on the particular ideas that might be in the passage. The title of this article gives me a few clues. I'm interested in reading it because I'm curious about polar bears. The word "nation" in the title is a little confusing though. It makes me wonder if this article is going to be about where polar bears live. (Enter "Where do polar bears live?" in the second column of the chart.) I also wonder if this passage might be about what it's like for people to live in nations where it is very cold, and not so much about polar bears. (Enter "living in really cold countries?"). *These two questions will be enough to focus my attention as I start reading. I hope this article is about polar bears!*

Note:
You can write out the full question if you believe students need to see that modeled, or you can demonstrate that it can save time to use notes that convey the full question, rather than writing out the full question each time.

QAR Reading Cycle Chart

QAR	MY QUESTIONS	MY ANSWERS
BEFORE-READING QUESTIONS		
On My Own	What do I know about polar bears?	
Author & Me	Where do polar bears live?	
Author & Me	Living in really cold countries?	

Read the first two sentences of the text for further information and, based on this, model refining your questions to focus your reading. Comment that you found out that this passage will describe the Gilbert triplets and their mission, so you know it is about polar bears. You are going to use what you've read to create questions to focus your attention during reading.

Step **3** GUIDED PRACTICE

Ask students to help you ask questions to guide the reading of the next section of text. Refer to the reading cycle poster and remind students that during-reading, questions are usually Author & Me, Think & Search, with only one or two Right There QARs. Questions will vary, but possible questions are in the chart.

> *Based on what we know about the article so far, think about the kinds of questions that it would be helpful to ask next.*

Model by suggesting one or two questions, then elicit questions from students, discussing the QARs that each represents, then adding the questions in the QAR Reading Cycle Chart, During-Reading section. Examples of QARs and questions include the following:

> ▶ Why are polar bears in danger of becoming extinct? [*Think & Search: Answer should make a link between climate change and the change in the polar bears' habitat, including access to food.*]

> ▶ What is the goal of the triplet's mission? [*Right There: spread awareness, raise money*]

Note:
The QAR to use in answering each question will not become visible until during reading. Initially, enter *only* the question in the chart. The QAR is determined as you read with the questions in mind and the answer is entered after reading.

Distribute a copy of the passage to each student and display the text section you will be reading aloud. Ask students to read along with you or listen carefully for information that will help you answer the questions on the class QAR Reading Cycle Chart. Enter the QAR in the chart, along with information that answers the questions.

QAR	MY QUESTIONS	MY ANSWERS
BEFORE-READING QUESTIONS		
Think & Search	Polar bears in danger? Why?	Global climate change causing ice to melt Habitat loss
Right There	Goal of the triplets mission?	Raise money and raise awareness

Step 4 COACHING

Tell students that they will be working with partners to create one or two additional questions to guide the reading of the next section of text. Note that the title of this section is "Taking Action" and that the question(s) they create will have something to do with this section header.

Give each student a blank copy of the QAR Reading Cycle Chart and have everyone enter the questions already listed on the class chart. Let students know that their questions should have something to do with the information in the header (e.g., "What kind of action are the triplets taking?" "What action should people take to help save the bears?" "What different kinds of action will help the polar bears?"). Ask students to write neatly, because pairs of students will be exchanging papers with one another.

Sample QARs, questions, and answers relevant to this section include, but aren't limited to, the following:

▶ What part do T-shirts play in the triplets' efforts? [*Think & Search: Answer includes information related to the T-shirt project for creating awareness and raising funds: the design/logo, donating portion of the profits, response from orders and television (CNN) features.*]

▶ What can I do to help with this mission? [*Author & Me: Possible answer is purchase a T-shirt, spread awareness.*]

When partners have finished this task, ask them to exchange their papers with another pair and use that pair's questions to guide their reading. Have them enter the answers they were able to locate on the QAR Reading Cycle Chart and indicate the QAR they used in answering.

Then have partners briefly discuss new questions they can add to the class chart. Let a few pairs share questions they found helpful in supporting their text understanding, indicating the QAR and the useful information from the text. Use students' additional questions to underscore the importance of Think & Search and Author & Me questions, and the limited information one gathers when answering Right There questions. Emphasize that valuable Right There QARs are those that focus on critically important information.

Step **5** INDEPENDENT APPLICATION

Have partners return their classmates' copies of the QAR Reading Cycle Chart. Then tell students that they will be working on their own to create questions to guide their reading of the final section of text. Refer to the new head, "Looking Ahead," and the reading cycle poster. Remind students that during reading, questions are usually Author & Me, Think & Search, and Right There. After reading, questions are Author & Me.

Based on what we have learned about the polar bears and the triplets' project so far, think about the kinds of questions that it would be helpful to ask next, given that the heading is "Looking Ahead." Start by creating one during-reading question you think would be useful in focusing your attention on the content that is signaled by this heading. Then, when you have finished reading the passage, create two after-reading questions we can use in our closing discussion to connect what we've learned to our own lives. You will be sharing your work with another student, so please write neatly.

AFTER READING

Step **6** SELF-ASSESSMENT & GOAL SETTING

Have students exchange their questions with a partner. Give them time to work with the original questions, as well as the new ones they and their partner generated. They should enter any useful new information in the third column of the QAR Reading Cycle Chart.

Bring students together to share a few after-reading questions. Help them make connections to what they have learned about the plight of the polar bears, the triplets' work to save the bears, and what each of us might do to help.

Display the I Can Statement and ask students to keep the statement in mind as they discuss what they learned in today's lesson. Focus them on the ways in which questioning helps readers' understanding and the way they used the title, headings, and their own interest to create questions to guide their reading. After several students have shared their ideas, summarize by reminding them that asking appropriate questions before, during, and after reading will help them better comprehend and enjoy the text.

Close by asking students to complete the QAR Self-Assessment Thinksheet and turn it in with their finished QAR Reading Cycle Chart.

Polar Bear Nation

By Kristin Lewis

For use with
Step 2: Modeling

title and the first
paragraph

Connor, Hayley, and Emma Gilbert are 16-year-old triplets on a mission: They want to save polar bears from extinction—and they're doing it one T-shirt at a time.

For use with
Step 3: Guided
Practice

next
2 paragraphs

Polar bears roam the Arctic ice in the northernmost parts of the world. But global climate change is causing the ice to melt—and that's bad news for these majestic creatures. That's why the Gilberts decided to start Polar Bear Nation. Their goal is to raise money for and awareness of the polar bear's plight.

Earlier this year [2008], the U.S. government put polar bears on the "threatened species" list of the Endangered Species Act. The bears are the first animals to make the list because of anticipated habitat loss from global warming. While the decision is a step in the right direction, conservationists like the Gilberts worry it isn't enough.

Taking Action

For use with
Step 4: Coaching

"Taking Action"
section

When the triplets' dad, a photojournalist, returned from a trip to the Arctic in 2006, the teens were shocked to learn how dire the situation is for polar bears.

"They're a great species to show climate change because here we have this bear that has been surviving in the harshest environment on the planet and what we're doing in our daily lives is going to kill them," says Connor. "It's already begun with some bears reverting to cannibalism and the number of cubs falling off."

Polar bears hunt seals, their main food source, from atop sea ice. As warmer temperatures cause the ice to melt, the bears have fewer places to catch their dinner.

While most of these colossal animals aren't in immediate danger, they soon will be if things don't change. A United States Geological Survey study last year estimated that polar bears could disappear by the year 2050.

Connor, Hayley, and Emma put their heads together and came up with an idea. Why not start a clothing line and donate a portion of the profit to Polar Bears International, a nonprofit organization that works to preserve the bear's habitat?

They designed a line of T-shirts, sweats, and sweatshirts called Polar Bear Nation. The name and logo depict the five nations where polar bears reside: the U.S. (Alaska), Canada, Russia, Norway, and Greenland (administered by Denmark).

"When we wear Polar Bear Nation shirts, people ask 'Oh what's that?' and then we have an opportunity to tell them," says Connor. "It's a great way to get into other people's lives with the message."

Since launching the clothing line last year, the response has been overwhelming. Besides the U.S., the triplets get orders from Australia, Denmark, and Canada. CNN even featured them on its *Young People Who Rock* show. "It's great because we're bringing the world together," Connor says.

Looking Ahead

For use
with Step 5:
Independent
Application

"Looking Ahead"
section

The triplets have big plans for Polar Bear Nation. They recently launched a Web site, polarbearnation.org, to create an international community of polar bear conservationists. "We've always envisioned it to become a group of citizens of the world," says Connor. "We want this whole group to be like a social network—a group of people who are empowered to create change."

When it comes to creating change, the Gilberts have strong ideas about how every person can help stop global warming and save the polar bear's habitat. The first step is to use less energy. That means sharing car rides with friends, taking public transportation, turning off lights when you leave a room, and unplugging electronics when not in use.

"The little things you do in your daily life add up. That's the point a lot of people miss," says Connor. "People say, 'Oh I don't have the power to curb global warming; it's too huge for me.' But if everyone does a little bit, you can make a real change."

Questioning With Narrative Text

GOAL • Help students understand how to generate and respond to questions appropriate to each phase of the reading cycle

I Can Statement

I can ask and answer appropriate questions before, during, and after reading.

Reading Cycles & QARs

Reading Cycles: Before, During, and After Reading

QARs: *Right There:* Identifying important information

Think & Search: Connecting ideas across text

Author & Me: Making text-to-self connections

On My Own: Brainstorming prior to reading

Materials *(See CD for reproducibles.)*

▶ "Watermelon War" by Michael Priestley (narrative passage), p. 106 (one copy for each student)

▶ Core QARs Poster (display copy)

▶ QAR and the Reading Cycle Poster (display copy)

(Refer to the posters as necessary during lesson.)

▶ QAR Reading Cycle Chart (display copy and one for each pair and for each student)

▶ QAR Self-Assessment Thinksheet (one copy for each student)

Step **1** EXPLICIT EXPLANATION

Tell students that, most of the time, questioning in school means answering questions the teacher or the text has asked. However, we often learn as much, if not more, by creating our own questions as we read.

> *Today I'm going to teach you how to ask—not just answer—appropriate questions before, during, and after reading. The focus of today's lesson is on how to use these questions strategically throughout the reading cycle.*

Step **2** MODELING

Display the QAR Reading Cycle Chart. Tell students that you will be using the QAR Reading Cycle Chart to help you keep track of three things: (1) the questions you have created for each phase of the reading cycle, (2) the QAR you think will be most helpful in answering the question, and (3) the information you think would contribute to a good answer to the question.

Display the QAR and the Reading Cycle Poster. Remind students that different QARs go best with different phases of the reading cycle. Elicit the three phases (or, if necessary, prompt students using the poster). Have students explain why the QARs identified in the poster are appropriate to that particular phase of the reading cycle. Guide them to remember or understand the cycle: generating background knowledge and prediction (On My Own/Author & Me) before reading, using text information and making connections during their reading (Right There, Think & Search, Author & Me), and reflecting on their connections to the text and its impact on their thinking after reading (Author & Me).

> **Note:**
> If students have completed Lessons 4 and 13, begin by reminding them to think about what they have learned about QARs and the reading cycle. Let students know that in this lesson, you are focusing on question-asking with narratives.

> *Active readers create questions that help them think more deeply about what they are reading. We've learned that before reading a new text or text section, questions help us brainstorm what we know or have experienced that relates to the story we're about to read, and questions focus our attention on the text. Another type of question relates to the content we expect from the type of text we are reading—for stories like the one we are reading today, we expect characters and plot. Another type of question helps us make connections between the story events or ideas and our own lives. And questions can help us*

review important ideas once we have finished reading a whole text. Questions support our understanding throughout the entire reading cycle.

Display a blank copy of the QAR Reading Cycle Chart.

Before I begin reading, I want to ask On My Own questions to brainstorm what I might already know or have experienced that will help me connect to the story I'm reading. I also want to ask Author & Me QARs that will help focus my attention by predicting what may happen in the story. (In the Before-Reading Questions section of the chart, enter "On My Own" under QAR in one line and "Author & Me" in the next.) I'm going to use the QAR Reading Cycle Chart to organize my questions and keep track of my answers.

I'll start by looking at the title of the piece, "Watermelon War," and think about what I know about watermelons and war that could help me understand the text. I'm imagining what a watermelon war could be. (Write notes to convey the question as you think aloud.) Does a watermelon war involve a fight using watermelons, a fight over watermelons, or something else?

> **Note:**
> Demonstrate that it can save time to use notes that convey the question, rather than writing out the full question each time.

Next I'd like to create an Author & Me question for predicting what this text is about, but I don't have enough clues yet from the author to help me do more than brainstorm. I'm going to see if there is a clue in the first and second sentence of the story that can help me create an Author & Me QAR to focus on what the story is about.

QAR Reading Cycle Chart

QAR	MY QUESTIONS	MY ANSWERS
BEFORE-READING QUESTIONS		
On My Own	Fighting with watermelons? Fighting over watermelons? Something else?	
Author & Me		

BEFORE READING   **DURING READING**   AFTER READING

Read the first two sentences in the first paragraph aloud. Then model that you have enough information to create on Author & Me QAR to focus your reading.

Ah, these clues are just what I need to create a good Author & Me question to focus my attention on what might happen in the story. I'm going to ask,

What kind of competition are Chet and Lou having over watermelons? (Enter question or notes for question in the Before-Reading Author & Me row of the QAR Reading Cycle Chart).

Continue reading the remainder of the first two paragraphs.

Spend a brief amount of time having students discuss possible answers to the two questions and how the questions helped focus their attention on certain text ideas.

Step **3** GUIDED PRACTICE

Encourage students to help you ask questions to guide the reading of the next section of text. Refer to the reading cycle poster and remind students that during reading, good questions usually are mostly Think & Search and Author & Me, with one or two Right There QARs to help remember important ideas. Questions will vary, but potential questions are in the chart below.

> **Note:**
> The QAR to use in answering each question will not become visible until during reading. Initially, enter only the question. The QAR is determined as you read with the questions in mind.

QAR	MY QUESTIONS	MY ANSWERS
DURING-READING QUESTIONS		
Think & Search	How do Lou and Chet's reasons for growing the watermelons differ?	Chet: win the prize; Lou: the challenger & learn something new
Right There	What was the Grand Prize?	$300 for biggest watermelon
Think & Search	How did finding the newspaper article lead to a watermelon war?	Lou found the article, shared with Chet, different reasons for growing watermelons surfaced, led to competing to grow the biggest watermelon and not being friends
Author & Me	If I were a friend of Lou and Chet's, what would I choose to grow?	[Answers will vary.]

Notice that information for answering each of the questions may not be included in the current section of the text (e.g., "war" has not yet started). Maintain the QAR Reading Cycle Chart throughout the lesson, adding questions in each section as they arise, noting information for answering questions as you and the students encounter relevant ideas while reading.

> *Based on what we know about the story so far, think about the kinds of questions that would be helpful to ask next. Since this is a story, we need to ask questions that will focus our attention on the characters, setting, problem, and important events.*

> *Model by suggesting one or two questions yourself, then elicit questions from students, discussing the QAR used to generate these questions. Write the QARs and questions in the During-Reading Questions section of the chart.*

Distribute a copy of the passage to each student. Tell students to read along with you or listen carefully for information that will help you answer these questions. After reading this section, briefly discuss the answers to questions for which there was information available, and note questions for which information is still needed. Possible information to highlight is identified for each question in the chart above. Emphasize how having questions can help readers focus and remember important information about the setting, characters, the problem, and how it is resolved.

STEP **4** COACHING

Tell students that they will be working with partners to create questions to guide the reading of the next section of text. Give each pair a blank copy of the QAR Reading Cycle Chart. Have students refer to the reading cycle poster to remind them that during reading, the QARs are generally Author & Me and Think & Search, with only a few Right There.

> *Based on what we know about the story so far, think about the kinds of questions that it would be helpful to ask next. Remember, since this is a story, you will want to ask questions that focus on the characters, settings, problem, or important events. After you have generated your own questions, you can look at the class chart to see if there are any unanswered questions you want to add to your list. You will be exchanging papers with another pair of students, so be sure to write neatly.*

When partners have finished this task, ask them to exchange their questions with another pair and use each other's questions to guide their reading. Have them enter the answers they were able to find on the QAR Reading Cycle Chart. When they have finished, tell them to discuss which questions were most useful for helping them understand the problems that Chet and Lou were beginning to face, the challenges to their friendship, or the impact the contest was having on their relationship.

Draw on student-generated questions to illustrate the importance of Think & Search and Author & Me questions, and the limited information one gathers when answering

Right There questions. Emphasize that valuable Right There QARs are ones that focus on critically important information. Enter good examples of student-generated questions, representing different QARs, in the class QAR Reading Cycle Chart. Questions will vary but potential questions include:

▶ Who do you think is being a real friend? [*Author & Me: Lou, for being willing to help Chet, who didn't know anything about gardening*]

▶ Where did Chet get the information he needed to grow watermelons? [*Think & Search: library, Internet research*]

▶ Why were the two boys' parents worried? [*Right There: Contest could cost them their friendship even after it ends.*]

▶ Who do you think stands the better chance of winning the contest? [*Author & Me: Could be Lou: already knows what to do and could give tips to Chet, becomes determined once he sees Chet's attitude won't change; Could be Chet: really determined to win and willing to do research to figure out what watermelon plants need to grow. Both boys have successful plants.*]

Step 5 INDEPENDENT APPLICATION

Make sure each student has a copy of the QAR Reading Cycle Chart with space for entering during-and-after reading questions. Tell them that they will be working on their own to create questions to guide their reading of the final section of text. Refer again to the reading cycle poster and remind them that during reading, questions are usually Author & Me, Think & Search, and Right There. After reading, questions are Author & Me.

Based on what you know about the story so far, think about the kinds of questions that would be helpful to ask next. Since this is the last section of the story, you need to ask during-reading questions that focus on the characters, problem, important events, and if there is one, the solution to the problem. You will also need to create after-reading questions we can use in our closing discussion to connect the theme of the story to our own lives.

After you have generated your own questions, you can look at the class chart to see if there are any unanswered questions you want to add to your list. You will be sharing your work with another student, so please write neatly.

Sample questions for the final section are shown below:

During Reading

▶ What surprising turn happened that changed the outcome of the watermelon war? [*Think & Search: storm, tree fell down ruining Lou's watermelons, Chet put friendship ahead of competition*]

- Why was Mrs. Sadowski trying not to smile too much? [*Author & Me: Parents were happy that the boys had restored their friendship.*]

- What were Lou's feelings when he heard his mom say Chet was at his house and then saw him with the watermelon? [*Author & Me: Answers will vary.*]

After Reading

- How did Lou and Chet's views about friendship change over the course of the story? [*Author & Me: Answers will vary.*]

- If you were Chet, what might you have said to Lou when he refused any help? [*Author & Me: Answers will vary.*]

- If you were Lou, how would you have felt when Chet saw him bring over his largest watermelon? [*Author & Me: Answers will vary.*]

- What do you think the author of this story might have wanted you to think about as a result of reading about Lou, Chet, and the watermelon wars? [*Author & Me: Answers will vary.*]

AFTER READING

Step 6 SELF-ASSESSMENT & GOAL SETTING

Have students exchange their questions with a partner and discuss one during-reading question and one after-reading question from each person's chart. Then bring the class together. Ask two or three students to share their during-reading questions, and two or three share their after-reading questions. Enter these questions on the class chart.

Display the I Can Statement and ask students to keep the statement in mind as they discuss what they learned in today's lesson. Focus students on the ways in which questioning helps readers' understanding. After several students have shared their ideas, summarize by reminding them that asking appropriate questions before, during, and after reading will help them better comprehend and enjoy the text.

Close by asking students to share how they might use this strategy—asking questions throughout the reading cycle—across the school day and outside of school. Have students complete the QAR Self-Assessment Thinksheet and turn it in with their completed QAR Reading Cycle Chart and responses to the questions.

Watermelon War

By Michael Priestley

For use with
Step 2: Modeling
title and the first
2 paragraphs

All summer, Chet Murphy and Lou Sadowski were locked in a tense competition. Their parents named it the Watermelon War. They watched it play out for ten long weeks. Then suddenly, the Watermelon War ended in an unexpected way.

Until the Watermelon War started, Chet and Lou got along fine. They often talked and joked over the fence between their yards. Chet practiced tricks on his bike, and Lou tended his garden. Every fall, Chet helped Lou rake up the leaves from the huge oak in the Sadowskis' backyard. Lou always repaid Chet with a jar of homemade salsa. He made it with tomatoes from his garden.

For use with
Step 3: Guided Practice
next
7 paragraphs

The trouble started on a June morning. Chet was in his driveway pumping air into his bicycle tires. Meanwhile, Lou was getting his garden ready for planting. As he dug his trowel into the soil, Chet's face appeared over the fence.

"Hey, Lou," Chet began, "you'd better grow some great tomatoes this summer. I've got a craving for your salsa."

Lou grinned and shook his head. "Sorry, Chet, I'm switching to watermelons this year."

"Why watermelons?" asked Chet.

Lou pulled a folded-up newspaper article from his pocket and passed it over the fence. Chet unfolded it and read the heading. It said, "Gardeners' Club Holds Watermelon Contest." As Chet skimmed the article, one detail caught his eye. "A $300 Grand Prize goes to the person who grows the biggest watermelon by September 1st."

"Three hundred dollars!" Chet exclaimed. "That could get me to grow watermelons."

"I'm more interested in the challenge than the prize," Lou replied. "I know how to grow tomatoes. Now I want to learn something new."

For use with
Step 4: Coaching
next
4 paragraphs

Soon Chet was speeding toward Marv's Garden Center on his bike. He bought a package of watermelon seeds and then rode back home. Chet didn't know anything about gardening. He could never win the contest. Still, Lou decided, if Chet wanted his help, Lou would give it.

As the days passed, however, it became obvious that Chet did not want help. When Lou offered tips, Chet waved him off. Instead, he borrowed gardening books from the library. He did research on the Internet, too. Chet was determined to win the contest. But he didn't want to share the credit—or the prize money—with Lou. Once Lou realized how much Chet wanted to win, his attitude about the contest changed. Lou decided that he wanted to win, too.

As the days stretched into weeks, leafy watermelon plants sprouted in each boy's garden. Before long, flowers blossomed on the vines and then fell off. In their place, small, green fruits began to grow. Slowly and steadily, the watermelons grew larger.

Chet and Lou often tended their patches at the same time, but they no longer chatted over the fence. The boys' silence bothered their parents. They worried that, no matter how the contest turned out, hard feelings between the boys would linger.

Then the Watermelon War took a surprising turn. It was a hot day in late August. Chet and Lou were tending their watermelons. Then the sky suddenly darkened and the wind kicked up. Thunder boomed in the distance. Rain started falling as the boys scurried into their houses.

For use with Step 5: Independent Application

remainder of passage

CRACK! THUD! A gust of wind snapped a large branch from the Sadowskis' oak tree. As it crashed to the ground, the branch fell across Lou's garden. It flattened every single watermelon.

Lou watched the destruction from a window. He felt sick with disappointment. His hard work and hopes had come to nothing. Lou shut himself in his bedroom. At dinnertime, he refused to eat.

The doorbell rang a while later. Lou could hear his mother greeting Chet. Then she called out, "Lou, Chet has brought something for you."

When Lou reached the door, he saw Chet holding a huge watermelon. "Hey, Lou," Chet laughed, "I need your help eating this watermelon. It's the biggest one in my patch."

"Why would you eat it now?" asked Lou. "The contest isn't over."

"When I saw what happened to your patch," Chet explained, "the contest didn't matter so much anymore. It's not as important as staying friends with you."

Trying not to smile too much, Mrs. Sadowski took the watermelon from Chet. She cut it into slices and arranged them on a platter.

Monitoring Comprehension of Informational Text

GOAL ● Help students monitor their comprehension and use strategies to repair comprehension failures

I Can Statement

I can monitor my comprehension during reading and use QAR knowledge and tools to help me fix comprehension problems.

Reading Cycle & QARs

Reading Cycle: During Reading

QARs: *Right There:* Underscore important details

Think & Search: Locate and organize information

Author & Me: Make predictions and draw inferences to support comprehension

Materials *(See CD for reproducibles of all materials.)*

▶ "Deep Sea Disguise" by Stephanie Smith (informational passage), p. 116 (one copy for each student)

▶ Core QARs Poster (display copy)

▶ QAR and the Reading Cycle Poster (display copy)

(Refer to the posters as necessary during lessons.)

▶ QAR Monitoring Chart (display copy, one copy for each pair and for each student)

▶ QAR Fix-Up Strategies Poster

▶ QAR Self-Assessment Thinksheet (one copy for each student)

Step **1** EXPLICIT EXPLANATION

Introduce the lesson by explaining what monitoring is and why it's important. Lead students to understand that monitoring enables them to do the following:

▶ Check to see that they are comprehending the text

▶ Recognize when there is a problem with comprehension

▶ Use the right strategy from their toolkit to fix the problem

Today I will be teaching you about monitoring, an important comprehension strategy that is used during reading. When I monitor my comprehension, I check to make sure that I'm gaining a good understanding of the text.

When I read and the ideas all make sense, I experience what can be called the "click" of comprehension: My reading is just clicking along! My reading is going well, and I find that I have a good understanding of the text. In that situation, I don't really think about strategies or slow down my reading to use a particular tool that I know about—I just keep reading.

However, every now and then I have a different experience. My reading isn't clicking along. Instead, it's more like a big comprehension "clunk." Something in the text is creating a comprehension problem for me, and my understanding breaks down.

When I recognize that I've run into a problem with comprehension—a clunk—I need to do something to fix the problem so I can get my comprehension clicking again.

Often, all I have to do to fix the problem is keep reading. In this strategy, we keep reading because the author has put a question in our mind and is going to answer it later in the text. Sometimes, I can go back and reread a section because I just skipped something or read something wrong and rereading helps me fix the problem.

But other times I realize that I have to do more than just continuing to read or slowing down and rereading. When this happens, I use one or more of the QAR tools we've been learning about (refer to the QAR Fix-Up Strategies Poster).

Ask students to think about the QAR tools they learned about in previous lessons (e.g., QAR Think & Search Important Information Chart, QAR Author & Me Inference Chart, QAR and the Reading Cycle Poster). Lead a discussion of how these tools helped them comprehend text during the lessons and the ways they used the tools in other situations, in or out of school.

Display the QAR Monitoring Chart. Explain to students that using this chart can help them monitor comprehension during reading and choose the tools to fix comprehension problems that may occur.

> *When I run into a comprehension problem—or clunk—I'll enter it in the second column of our QAR Monitoring Chart so I can keep the problem in mind. In the third column, I'll write the question and the possible QAR it represents so I can think about which source of information might be most relevant. To fill in the fourth column, I'll think of a QAR tool, such as those we just discussed, to help me fix the problem. I can always decide that the tool is to keep on reading, but I like having some other options in case that doesn't fix the problem. In the last column, I'll write the answer to my question. Taking these steps will help me fix my comprehension problem, so I can continue reading.*

BEFORE READING   **DURING READING**   AFTER READING

Step **2** MODELING

Display the text, "Deep Sea Disguise." As you proceed through the text, use the coding convention from Lessons 9 and 11: an exclamation point (!) for ideas that you suspect are important, one question mark (?) for ideas that might be important, and a new code, three question marks (???), for ideas that might be important and that you don't understand right now.

> *I'm going to use the coding system we learned earlier to monitor my comprehension. I'll use an exclamation point for information that I think is important and a question mark for information that might be important. I'll use a new code, three question marks, for information that might be important but that I don't understand right now. The information I code with three question marks will go on our QAR Monitoring Chart.*

Proceed with a think-aloud such as the following.

> *"Deep Sea Disguise"—that's the title. I'm going to put three question marks next to it. This information seems important, but I don't understand what "deep sea disguise" means. This is my first possible comprehension problem, which I will enter on our QAR Monitoring Chart. (Write the information in the second column of the chart, as shown below.)*

My question is, "What is the meaning of the title 'Deep Sea Disguise?'" I suspect that the QAR is Author & Me and that I'll need to use the author's clues to identify useful background knowledge I may have. (Write the information in the third column of the chart, as shown below.) *I think a good tool to use would be the QAR Author & Me Prediction Chart. I don't have to make a whole chart. Instead, I can just make some notes using the categories I remember from that chart: Author, Me, Prediction.* (Write that information in the fourth column of the chart, as shown below).

QAR Monitoring Chart

	POSSIBLE COMPREHENSION PROBLEM	QUESTION AND QAR	TOOL TO FIX THE PROBLEM	ANSWER TO QUESTION
Section: 1	Title—"Deep Sea Disguise"—not sure what this means	Why did the author use the title "Deep Sea Disguise?" (Author & Me)	Author & Me Prediction Chart: Author: Deep sea plus disguise Me: Animals live in the deep sea, animals disguise themselves to avoid predators. Prediction: Might be about deep sea animals who disguise themselves to survive	

Tell students that you don't know the answer to your question yet, so you can't write anything in the last column. You will have to read on to see if your prediction is correct.

Read the first three paragraphs aloud and code the information as students follow along. Potential sites for coding include the following:

▶ Important (!): Sharks, fearing sharks, do not pose a major threat to humans.

▶ Might be important (?): Sharks have a distinct fin. Sharks have killed and attacked many people. People are not part of a shark's diet.

▶ Not clear (???): People have been killed by sharks, but it says sharks aren't a major threat. (Note: Convey to students that this is an example of conflicting information in the text.)

Conclude that you will need to add a new prediction as the article doesn't seem to be about disguises, but it does seem to be about whether or not sharks are dangerous to humans. Cross out your earlier prediction and write a new one: *probably about how sharks aren't a major threat to people.*

Step 3 GUIDED PRACTICE

Distribute a copy of the QAR Monitoring Chart to each student along with a copy of the text.

> *Please follow along carefully as I read the next section of text aloud. As I read, I want you to code the information.* (Review the three coding symbols. Emphasize that information coded ??? might go on the class QAR Monitoring Chart.)

As you read, pause after each phrase or sentence to give students a chance to code the text. When you have finished reading this section, briefly discuss with students the information they coded with an exclamation point or question mark. Have them give reasons for their choices.

Then move on to a discussion of the information that students chose to code with three question marks. Candidates for "???" include the following: "he goes wild," how a reputation can be fueled (this metaphor may not be clear to students), "great white."

The sample chart entry below is based on a possible comprehension problem posed by the phrase "he goes wild." If you use this example, you can make the connection to the problem triggered by the title, "Deep Sea Disguise." Point out that you now have the information to answer the first question in the chart. Add the answer to the chart: "title refers to Cousteau's use of submarine disguised as shark."

	POSSIBLE COMPREHENSION PROBLEM	QUESTION AND QAR	TOOL TO FIX THE PROBLEM	ANSWER TO QUESTION
Section: 2	He "goes wild"—unclear what this means	How can Fabien Cousteau help people understand about sharks by going wild? (Author & Me)	Author & Me Inference Chart: Author: Cousteau "goes wild" to accomplish his mission. Me: "Going wild" usually means acting in a crazy way—doesn't make sense in this context. Inference: "Going wild" could have a different meaning.	Cousteau studies sharks by using a submarine shaped like a shark. "Going wild" means he disguises himself like a shark, a wild animal.

Continue with other examples of comprehension clunks that students have identified.

Step 4 COACHING

Give each student a blank copy of the QAR Monitoring Chart.

> *You and a partner will read the third section of this passage together and code the information as we have been doing.*

If students require a review of the codes, provide them with a reminder.

> *When you and your partner have finished coding, look back for information in the text that you coded with three question marks. These are the clunks, or possible comprehension problems. Choose one possible comprehension problem and enter it in your QAR Monitoring Chart. Figure out the question you have about this information and the likely QAR for it. Then think about the tool you can use to fix the problem. If you can answer the question, go ahead and write it. But as you've seen, we don't always learn the answers to our questions right away.*

Give partners time to read the text and discuss possible comprehension problems. Circulate among them and provide assistance as needed.

If students tell you that they did not code any text information with three question marks, ask them to return to the text and identify a place that they think might be confusing to other readers, even if it was not confusing to them.

Here is a sample of an entry for this section of the text.

	POSSIBLE COMPREHENSION PROBLEM	QUESTION AND QAR	TOOL TO FIX THE PROBLEM	ANSWER TO QUESTION
Section: 3	Sub has no engine.	How can the sub move if it has no engine? (Right There or Think & Search)	Keep reading	Sub uses air pressure to move.

Have each pair form a square with another pair (four students). Ask squares to compare and contrast their possible comprehension problems, questions and QARs, tools for fixing the problem, and any answers. As you circulate among the students, be on the lookout for two or three pairs who have done a good job with the task.

Bring the whole class together. Call on the pairs you identified earlier to share their charts and their thinking. You may collect partners' work to informally evaluate the class's progress, but we recommend using the individual work from Step 5 to evaluate student learning.

Step **5** INDEPENDENT APPLICATION

Tell students that they will now work individually to read the final section of the passage. When they have finished coding, they should look back and choose a possible comprehension problem to enter in their QAR Monitoring Chart. Then they should fill in the question and QAR, the possible tool, and the answer, if it is available.

Here is a sample entry for this section of the text.

	POSSIBLE COMPREHENSION PROBLEM	QUESTION AND QAR	TOOL TO FIX THE PROBLEM	ANSWER TO QUESTION
Section: 4	Sharks at top of ocean food chain	What does it mean to be at the top of the food chain? (Right There, Think & Search?)	Keep reading	Answer not found—need to look in another source

As in Step 4, move around the room and see if you can identify two or three students who are doing a good job with the task.

Bring the whole class together. Call on the students you identified earlier to share their charts and their thinking.

Note:
The above example illustrates the situation in which the comprehension problem cannot be fixed on the spot because the answer is not in the text being read. Instead, the reader will have to turn to another source, perhaps another book or the Internet. Be sure students know they may well encounter comprehension problems in informational text that require them to refer to another source.

Step 6 SELF-ASSESSMENT & GOAL SETTING

Display the I Can Statement and ask students to keep the statement in mind as they think about what they have learned.

> *Let's talk about what you learned about monitoring and how it helped you understand the text. Who would like to share something he or she learned?*

Elicit several student responses and build on these responses to review the tools or actions that you and the students identified as useful for fixing comprehension problems. These tools or actions may include the following: QAR Author & Me Prediction Chart, QAR Author & Me Inference Chart, reading further in the text, and looking for another source of information. Conclude the discussion by encouraging students to apply comprehension monitoring in other settings.

> *Describe how you can use the strategy of comprehension monitoring in other areas and how you can add this to your personal toolkit for reading. Please complete your QAR Self-Assessment Thinksheet and turn it in with your QAR Monitoring Chart.*

Deep Sea Disguise

By Stephanie Smith

**For use with
Step 2: Modeling**

title and the first
3 paragraphs

When you think of sharks, what images come to mind? Do you picture big mouths full of sharp, pointy teeth? Do you see a triangle-shaped fin sticking out of the water— a distinct sign of the feared creature lurking beneath?

If those scary images come to mind, you're not alone. Many people fear sharks— and for an understandable reason: Sharks have attacked and killed people. Such chilling events, which are often covered in the news, make many people worry about going back into the water.

But are sharks really the monsters many people believe them to be? People who study sharks say they are not. Sharks do not pose a major threat to humans, experts say. People are not part of a shark's regular diet. For this reason, the chances of being attacked by a shark are very slim. In 2004, there were just 61 unprovoked shark attacks worldwide.

**For use with
Step 3: Guided
Practice**

next
3 paragraphs
and map

Explorer Fabien Cousteau (coo-**stow**) wants to show people that sharks are not mindless killers, but interesting creatures that deserve respect and care. To carry out his mission, he goes wild.

Cousteau uses a submarine that is shaped like a shark to study one of the most feared shark species—the great white (see map). In the past, most shark researchers have used bait to attract sharks or watched them from a metal cage. Those practices lead sharks to attack, Cousteau says, and help fuel their bad reputations. He wants people to see a great white's more brainy, personal side.

"If I can document the learning ability of the shark, I may be able to change our [idea] of them as villains. And if we understand them better, we will be better able to revere and protect them," explains Cousteau.

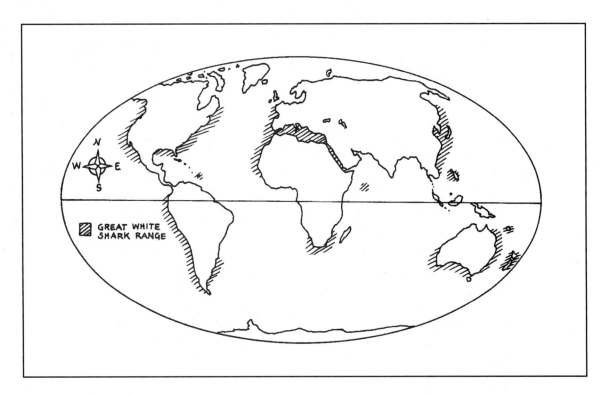

GREAT WHITE
SHARK RANGE

From Idea to Action

Fabien Cousteau is the grandson of famous ocean explorer Jacques Cousteau. But the idea for his shark sub didn't come from the family business. Fabien got the idea from a children's book he read when he was a kid growing up in Paris, France. (Cousteau now lives in New York City.) In the book, a boy uses a shark-shaped sub to explore the sea.

Cousteau's shark sub, named *Troy*, looks and moves a lot like a great white shark. The sub has no engine, which would make noise that might scare the real sharks away. Air pressure is used to push *Troy*'s tail back and forth, which moves the sub forward. Troy's eyes are camera lenses. Another camera, disguised to look like a fish, is on Troy's back.

While in *Troy*, Cousteau says he has seen great white sharks acting in ways that show their true character. Some sharks have puffed their gills, opened their mouths, and rolled their eyes at *Troy*. Cousteau says those are forms of communication. "I've had sharks [behave like] they do amongst themselves," he says.

For use
with Step 5:
Independent
Application

"Human Threat"
section

Human Threat

Cousteau says it's important for people to learn the true nature of sharks soon. Shark populations worldwide are dwindling. According to a study published in the journal *Nature* in 2003, large fish populations—including tuna and sharks—have dropped 90 percent in the last 50 years. Researchers blame the decline mostly on overfishing and accidental catches in big fishing nets.

That's bad news not just for sharks, but also for the ocean's ecosystems, Cousteau says. Sharks have lived in the seas for more than 400 million years and are at the top of the ocean's food chain. Losing them would affect every life form lower on the chain. Humans rely on the ocean's creatures for food. Many businesses, such as fishing and tourism, also depend on sea life.

By thinking of sharks as monsters that we might be happy to live without, Cousteau says, "we are doing a huge [disservice] to them and us."

Monitoring Comprehension of Narrative Text

GOAL • Help students monitor their comprehension and use strategies to repair comprehension failures

I Can Statement

I can monitor my comprehension during reading and use QAR knowledge and tools to help me fix comprehension problems.

Reading Cycle and QARs

Reading Cycle: During Reading

QARs: *Right There:* Identifying important information
Think & Search: Connecting ideas across text
Author & Me: Making text-to-self connections
On My Own: Brainstorming prior to reading

Materials *(See CD for reproducibles.)*

▶ "Blown Away" by Tony Smith (as told to John DiConsiglio) (narrative passage), p. 126 (one copy for each student)

▶ Core QARs Poster (display copy)

▶ QAR and the Reading Cycle Poster (display copy)

(Refer to posters as necessary during lessons.)

▶ QAR Monitoring Chart from Lesson 15 (one copy for each pair and for each student)

▶ QAR Fix-Up Strategies Poster (display copy)

▶ QAR Self-Assessment Thinksheet (one copy for each student)

Step **1** EXPLICIT INSTRUCTION

If students participated in Lesson 15, make the connection to it by explaining that today's lesson continues the focus on monitoring. If not, tell students that they will be learning about monitoring, an important comprehension strategy that active readers use during reading. Explain that monitoring helps active readers do three things. (**Note:** If you have taught Lesson 15, you may want to invite students to share what they remember from the lesson about these three monitoring actions.)

▶ Check during reading that what they are reading makes sense

▶ Recognize when comprehension is failing and potential reasons for the failure (e.g., word, text, or knowledge level)

▶ Use an appropriate tool from their toolkit of comprehension strategies to fix the problem

Display QAR Fix-Up Strategies Poster to review the QAR tools students now have in their toolkit from previous lessons (e.g., QAR Think & Search Important Information Chart, QARs, and the Reading Cycle Poster) and each tool's purpose. Explain that even active readers do not use all the tools all the time. Rather, active readers think about their purpose for reading, the tools they have available, and how to use a tool when they need to do so to ensure they will understand the text.

A think-aloud patterned after the one in Lesson 15 is included below. If you have taught Lesson 15, use students' performance in that lesson as the basis for your decisions about how much of this think-aloud to repeat, modify, or skip.

> *Today I will be teaching you about an important comprehension strategy that is used during reading—monitoring. Monitoring helps me decide when I need to use tools from my comprehension toolkit to help me better understand what I am reading. Monitoring helps me notice that much of the time my reading is going smoothly—I experience the "click" of comprehension. I can find information for my predictions, recognize important information, and draw inferences when I need to. In this case, I just keep reading along.*
>
> *Monitoring also helps me notice that I sometimes encounter comprehension problems when I read. Instead of a click, I experience a "clunk" of comprehension. I realize that the text is not making sense to me. When this happens, I need to slow down and reread. If I try rereading the text and find that it still doesn't make sense, I know that I need to go to my comprehension toolkit.*

Sometimes I've experienced a clunk because of a word or phrase I don't know— something that is Right There in the text that should help me isn't very useful. Sometimes I know all the words, but there's a lot to keep organized in my head. I find that I am confused or that I keep forgetting things I've just read. And sometimes I realize that while I know all the words, I don't know enough On My Own to make sense of what is in the text. So not all comprehension clunks occur for the same reasons.

Note:

In this lesson, we identify possible parts of the text that you can use to model comprehension monitoring: checking for understanding, recognizing problems, and then fixing these problems. Just one part of the text is presented as an example for each step of the lesson. We chose these examples to illustrate comprehension problems that might be fixed using different tools. Please feel free to use other parts of the text that may be a better match to the comprehension needs of your students.

Display the QAR Monitoring Chart (introduced in Lesson 15; make this connection if students participated in that lesson). Explain to students that using this chart can help them monitor comprehension during reading and learn to use tools to fix comprehension problems that may occur.

When I run into a comprehension problem, or clunk, I can enter the problem in the second column of the QAR Monitoring Chart. This helps me remember what caused the clunk. In the third column, I write the question I have and the possible QAR it represents so that I can think about which source of information might be most relevant. To fill in the fourth column, I think of a comprehension strategy tool, such as those we just discussed, to help me fix the problem. I can always decide that the tool is to keep on reading, but I like having some other options in case that doesn't fix the problem. In the last column, I write the answer to my question. Taking these steps helps me fix my comprehension problem, so I can continue reading.

DURING READING

STEP **2** MODELING

Display the passage, "Blown Away." As you proceed through the text, use the coding conventions from the lessons on Identifying Important Information (Lessons 9 and 11): *I'm going to use the coding system we learned earlier to monitor my comprehension. I'll use an exclamation point for information that I think is important and a question mark for information that might be important. I'll use a new code (or, if it's familiar from Lesson 15, "the new code"), three question marks, for information that might be important but that I don't understand right now. The information coded with three question marks is what I'll enter on our QAR Monitoring Chart.*

Proceed with a think-aloud such as the following.

> *The title of this narrative is "Blown Away." I'm going to put a question mark next to the title because I'm not sure yet what "blown away" means. I'll keep reading.*

> *The narrator is in a car, being driven through his town. But he can't believe what he's seeing. Let me put three question marks there, because it's unusual for someone to be in his own town and not believe his eyes. The rest of the paragraph describes things such as houses being blown on their sides. I'm going to put an exclamation point at the end of the paragraph because it seems important that so much damage occurred.*

> *I'm going to write about the possible comprehension problem of the narrator not believing his eyes. My question is, "What has happened to this town?" I suspect that the QAR is Author & Me and that I'll need to use the author's clues to identify useful background knowledge I may have. (Write the information in the third column of the chart, as shown below.)*

> *I think a good tool would be the QAR Author & Me Inference Chart. I don't have to make a whole chart. Instead, I can just make some notes using the categories I remember from it: Author, Me, Inference. (Write the information in the fourth column of the chart, as shown below.)*

QAR Monitoring Chart

	POSSIBLE COMPREHENSION PROBLEM	QUESTION AND QAR	TOOL TO FIX THE PROBLEM	ANSWER TO QUESTION
Section: 1	Narrator can't believe his eyes, lots of damage	What happened to this town? (Author & Me)	Author & Me Inference Chart: Author: houses blown on sides, other severe damage Me: Hurricanes and other storms can cause this kind of damage. Inference: Hurricane hit this town.	

Tell students that you made an inference but don't know if it's correct. Reading further should help you find out if it actually was a hurricane that caused the damage.

Step **3** GUIDED PRACTICE

Distribute a copy of the QAR Monitoring Chart to each student along with a copy of the passage.

> *Please follow along carefully as I read the next section of text aloud. As I read, I want you to code the information. Use an exclamation point for information you're quite sure is important and a question mark for information that you think might be important. Use our new code, three question marks, for information that might be important but is puzzling or confusing—that we don't understand enough about it at this time. Information coded with three question marks might go on our QAR Monitoring Chart.*

As you read this section of text aloud, pause after each phrase or sentence to give students a chance to code. When you have finished reading this section, briefly discuss the information students coded with an exclamation point or question mark. Have them give reasons for their choices. Students will most likely point out that the earlier inference about the hurricane proved to be correct. When this happens, add the answer to the chart.

Move on to a discussion of the information students chose to code with three question marks. Candidates for "???" include the following: "Charley happened," and "And it made us wonder if anything was ever going to be the same again."

The sample below is based on a possible comprehension problem posed by the second item above: "Narrator wonders if anything would ever be the same again."

	POSSIBLE COMPREHENSION PROBLEM	QUESTION AND QAR	TOOL TO FIX THE PROBLEM	ANSWER TO QUESTION
Section: 2	Narrator wonders if anything would ever be the same again.	What will happen to the narrator and others in Punta Gorda? (Author & Me)	Author & Me Inference Chart: Author: people's homes, lives destroyed Me: When a disaster happens, people try to help one another. Prediction: People will rebuild their homes, lives with help from others.	

Continue with other examples of comprehension clunks that students identified.

Step 4 COACHING

Give each student a blank copy of the QAR Monitoring Chart.

> *You will be working with a partner to read the third section of this story. Read the section together and code the information as we have been doing.* (Review the codes if necessary.)
>
> *When you and your partner have finished coding, look back for information in the text that you coded with three question marks. These are the clunks, or possible comprehension problems. Choose one possible comprehension problem and enter it in your QAR Monitoring Chart. Figure out the question you have about this information and the likely QAR for your question. Then think of the tool you can use to fix the problem. If you can answer the question, go ahead and write it in the chart. But as you've seen, we don't always learn the answers to our questions right away.*

Give partners time to read the text and discuss possible comprehension problems. Circulate among students and provide assistance as needed.

If some students tell you that they did not code any text information with three question marks, ask them to return to the text and identify a place that they think might be confusing to other readers, even if it was not confusing to them.

Here is a sample of an entry for this section of the text.

	POSSIBLE COMPREHENSION PROBLEM	QUESTION AND QAR	TOOL TO FIX THE PROBLEM	ANSWER TO QUESTION
Section: 3	Narrator and family weren't worried.	Why weren't people worried about the hurricane? (Right There, Think & Search)	Keep reading	Storms normal part of life on Florida coast

Have two pairs form a square (four students). Ask students in the squares to compare and contrast their possible comprehension problems, questions and QARs, tools for fixing the problem, and any answers. As you circulate among students, be on the lookout for two or three pairs who have done a good job with the task.

Bring the whole class together. Call on the pairs you identified earlier to share their charts and their thinking. You may collect partner's work to informally evaluate the class's progress, but we recommend using the individual work from Step 5 to evaluate student learning.

Step **5** INDEPENDENT APPLICATION

Tell students that they will now work individually to read the final section of the text. When they have finished coding, they should look back and choose a possible comprehension problem to enter in their QAR Monitoring Chart. Then they should fill in the question and QAR, the possible tool, and the answer, if it is available.

Here are samples of entries for this section of the text.

	POSSIBLE COMPREHENSION PROBLEM	QUESTION AND QAR	TOOL TO FIX THE PROBLEM	ANSWER TO QUESTION
Section: 4	Most were hunkered down at shelters.	What does hunkered down mean? (Right There)	keep reading	word not defined in story; look in dictionary or ask for help
	friends not at home, wonders if anybody is still living in town	What happened to the narrator's friends? (Right There)	keep reading	most friends are fine, minimal damage
	three more hurricanes but things are getting better	How does a town fix things so that a new hurricane won't destroy it again?	QAR Identifying Important Information Chart (maybe there are clues I'm missing and this can help me focus)	No answer in this passage, but I can find other articles on the Internet about recovering from hurricanes and find out more about it. My chart will come in handy when I read further.

As in Step 4, circulate around the room and see if you can identify students who are doing a good job with the task.

Bring the whole class together. Call on the students you identified earlier to share their charts and their thinking.

Point out to students that they may have encountered fewer comprehension clunks during the last part of the story. Ask for their ideas about why this happened. Guide students to understand that active readers may need to work hard to gain a good understanding at the beginning of a story. However, once readers are well into the story, are familiar with the author's point of view and the content so far, comprehension may simply click along. In the case of "Blown Away," the last part of the story may have been quite easy to read because the author continued to provide more details about what happened in Punta Gorda after Hurricane Charley. Emphasize, though, that when we read stories that give us a window into something that may not be unfamiliar, the story may raise questions toward the end that lead the reader to seek further information.

BEFORE READING   DURING READING   **AFTER READING**

Step 6 SELF-ASSESSMENT & GOAL SETTING

Display the I Can Statement and ask students to keep the statement in mind as they think about what they have learned.

> *Let's talk about what you learned about monitoring and how it helped you understand the text. Who would like to share something they learned?*

Elicit several responses and build on them to review tools or actions that you and the students identified as useful in fixing comprehension problems. These tools or actions may include the following: QAR Author & Me Prediction Chart, QAR Author & Me Inference Chart, reading further in the text, and looking a word up in the dictionary. Conclude the discussion by encouraging students to apply comprehension monitoring in other settings.

> *Describe how you can use the strategy of comprehension monitoring in other areas and how you can add this to your personal toolkit for reading. Please complete your QAR Self-Assessment Thinksheet and turn it in with your QAR Monitoring Chart.*

Blown Away

By Tony Smith

As told to John DiConsiglio

**For use with
Step 2: Modeling**

title and the first
paragraph

My father steered our pickup truck down Highway 17 into our hometown of Punta Gorda, Florida. I could barely believe what I saw. Telephone poles and trees were piled in the streets. Swinging power lines shot off sparks. Homes were blown on their sides. Wooden beams and shingles hung from tree branches.

**Use with
Step 3: Guided
Practice**

next
3 paragraphs

We passed a woman sitting on the side of the road. All four walls of her house were gone. She'd dragged her furniture—what was left of it—onto her front lawn in the rain. And she wept into her hands.

My hometown looked like a disaster movie. I thought, "What happened here?" But I knew the answer: Charley happened.

Hurricane Charley hit Punta Gorda like a bomb. In about five hours, it nearly wiped the little town off the map. It destroyed people's homes—and their lives. And it made us wonder if anything was ever going to be the same again.

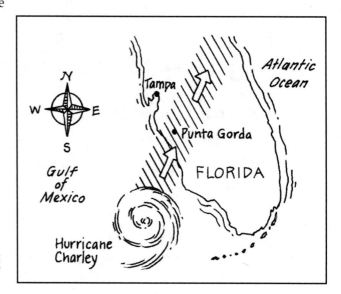

A Cozy Town

**Use with
Step 4: Coaching**

next
5 paragraphs

Before Charley struck, Punta Gorda was just a little town in southwest Florida, between Tampa and Fort Meyers. We're part of Charlotte County, a mix of farms, trailer parks, and antique houses. And I live here with my dad and my 11-year-old brother, Patrick. My mom passed away when I was 6. We're a close family. My dad even works at my high school cafeteria. There's not much to do here. For fun, I drive out to the mall in nearby Port Charlotte and hang with my friends.

We all knew Charley was coming. How could we not? It was on the news every night. But the weather reports said it would blow by us and hit Tampa. The night of the hurricane, my dad and I were house-sitting in Northport, a half hour away. My brother was out of town at our uncle's house. But we weren't worried. We hadn't even boarded up our windows. On the Florida coast, storms are just a normal part of life. We hadn't given Charley a second thought.

The Storm Hits

But Charley took an unexpected turn and slammed into Charlotte County. My dad and I stayed up all night listening to the radio. Just before sunrise, as the rain died down, we realized we had to get home. I knew it was going to be bad. But I never dreamed it'd be like this.

Punta Gorda was all but blown away. People were lucky if they had a roof and four walls. I was surprised to find my house still standing. The storm had ripped off the porch. And many of the windows were blown in. A live power wire hung in the middle of our driveway.

But we were among the lucky ones. We live across the street from a trailer park. Most of the trailers were demolished. Some had rolled upside down onto the highway. Others had their roofs and walls blown into our yard.

Use with Step 5: Independent Application

remainder of passage

As we drove through town, we saw few people. Most were hunkered down at shelters. Others huddled in tents or cars or under bridges. I tried calling my friends, but all the phones were down. I drove to each of their houses and left notes on their doors. "Is there anybody still living in this town?" I thought.

Torn to Shreds

Most of my friends made it through with minimal damage. My grandparents weren't so lucky. Their roof was torn to shreds. It's just like a sieve now, leaking water into their living room. The walls are covered in mold.

They're staying in a temporary trailer set up by FEMA, the Federal Emergency Management Agency. My grandmother cries all the time and asks, "What am I going to do? How am I going to start over?" I don't know what to tell her.

Three more hurricanes passed through Charlotte County in the weeks after Charley. Through our church, we tried to help others. We worked on people's homes, clearing away trees and debris. We helped make "blue roofs"—tarps stretched across the top of houses to keep the rain out.

Charlotte County was knocked around by the storms. But I can see signs of life. There are more people out on the streets now. My neighbors even manage a smile. Everyone says they're lucky to be alive. Strangers are helping pull trees off each other's yards. Stores are giving away everything from ice to diapers to sandwiches.

Charley leveled my school. It'll take two years to rebuild it. For now, I'm attending classes across town at Port Charlotte High. Half the kids go to school from 6 a.m. to 12:30. I start at 12:45 and end at 6 p.m. Before, Port Charlotte was our biggest football rival. But on our first day, I saw a welcome banner hung outside the school. Students gave up their desks and lockers for us. It's a little gesture. But it meant a lot. Charley tore the town apart—but it brought people together too.

Credits